Citations
Out of the Box

Frank G. Bennett

2013

Cover design by Titus Nemeth.

Typeset in LATEX from reStructuredText source. Citations generated by
citeproc-js driven by modified versions of zot4rst and citeproc-node.

ISBN 978-1479347711

for Mieko

In memoriam

Marion Clarice Bennett
née Springer

Teacher, life-counsellor
and beloved mother

Table of Contents

Foreword

by Lawrence Lessig[*]

Law is expensive. And inefficient. And too often, an embarrassment. Literally
— embarrassing. As a law professor and licensed attorney, I cringe when I
start my Prius, and am told that I need to click "I Agree" in order to use my
navigation system. Agree to what, I have no idea. Who has time to read such
junk? Likewise with my iPhone, which in its latest incarnation instructs me to
confirm that I have read and agreed to 68 pages of terms before I am permitted
to make a telephone call. Obviously, no one does what everyone affirms they
have done. Yet the law marches on, not really caring much that the world does
not conform to the fictions it creates.

I don't know why the obligation of efficiency has been lost in modern American law. I don't know when we lost the Holmesean instinct to throw silliness
away. But in domain after domain, lawyers tolerate the most ridiculous waste,
because no one within the law seems tasked with the job of eliminating it.

Legal citation is a perfect instance of this more general flaw. The dominant citation manual, The Bluebook, is a brilliant embarrassment. Hundreds of
pages long, with thousands of abbreviations, and convoluted rules specifying,
among other things, typeface variations — the system seems designed to punish
paralegals, or first year associates. Of course, it was not designed with those
purposes. And it is maintained by smart and decent souls aiming to do the best
they can. But whatever its virtues when invented, the system is an embarrassment in the 21st century. As anyone remotely familiar with the capabilities of
modern information technology recognizes, the idea that humans spin brain cy-
cles conforming to these rules is simply absurd. In 1974, things may have been
different. In the days before computers, a complex reference manual may have
made sense. But everything these citation manuals do computers could do better. The human brain was not invented/evolved/created (you pick) to waste its
time with silliness like this.

This book launches a platform that could help end this injustice. By building and implementing an open source uniform citation method, Frank Bennett
radically simplifies the process of citation, and encourages a generation of innovation on top of his own. With these tools, one can cite more simply today.
And with the platform launched today, this process will only get simpler still.
There will be a day when lawyers will no longer even remember that their legal
education included memorizing when small caps versus italics was required, or
how "legal" gets abbreviated.

---

[*]Roy L. Furman Professor of Law and Leadership at Harvard Law School, Director, Edmond J.
Safra Center for Ethics.

Getting to that day will not be simple. No doubt, there will be some who fight to preserve their particular bit of the inefficiency of today's system — sometimes because they can't imagine a better system, sometimes to preserve the rents the existing system gives them. We created uniform citation, these souls insist. We should have the right to control it.

But progress is the story of great innovations displaced. There was a time when credit card companies distributed weekly printed lists of stolen credit card numbers, and merchants compared a credit card to the pages on that booklet. Brilliant — for the time. But "common sense revolts at the idea," to borrow from Justice Douglas, that the creator of that idea might have the right to block the same task being performed by computers. George Eastman's company, Kodak, delivered a high quality and inexpensive technology for capturing images on film. That innovation was destroyed by digital imaging. I'm sure there's a legal memo in the archives of Kodak exploring ways to block (or control) the technology that eventually killed that great company. I'm sure the authors of that memo are hopeful history never finds it.

The law is expensive. It should be cheaper. The law is inefficient. It should feel the obligation that every competitive business does to change, and become more efficient. No doubt citation is a small bit of the inefficiency of law generally. But if we can't fix this, then the enterprise has indeed become hopeless.

I am not convinced it is hopeless. To the contrary, I am very hopeful that lawyers everywhere will embrace the platform Frank Bennett has launched, and extend it in ways that improve the work it is intended to achieve: a simple and practically costless way to point at the source that provides authority for your claim. His is not the only effort. Others are trying as well. But that is precisely the competition this system needs, so that someday, this completely mindless task might be done by something other than human minds.

Acknowledgements

Any project is a journey. This one began in the heat of personal pride, and has led by degrees to a cooler place: it has taught me to better appreciate the value of family and friendship, and the strength of community.

The chief subject of this book, Multilingual Zotero (MLZ), is a derivative work: most of its source code has been copied unabashedly from the Zotero reference manager. Thanks are due in the first instance to Dan Cohen and Sean Takats, who as co-Directors of the Roy Rosenzweig Center for History and New Media at George Mason University opted to release Zotero as free and open software. Without an open-source Zotero, MLZ would not exist.

The specific catalyst for the MLZ project itself was the Second Annual CiNII API Contest, organised by the Japan National Institute for Informatics in 2009. Looking at the announcement, Avram Lyon and I formed the naive notion that multilingual functionality could be added to Zotero in the few months remaining to the contest deadline. When our pitch to core Zotero developers Dan Stillman and Simon Kornblith yielded offers of server space and support, the project found its place in the garage; and with translation work by Tatsuki Sugiura and a little feedback from Shōji Kajita, we managed to get a presentable submission together. The judges were not impressed, unfortunately, but with rough code in place we had a foundation for further tinkering.

The plan to build robust legal support into MLZ was cast in a similar spirit of careless optimism. The initial response to this was muted—apart from some rather surprising legal rumblings. Professor Lessig kindly took time out from his busy schedule to help address these, and I am honoured to receive the Foreword to this volume from his hand. Thomas Bruce, Shigeru Kagayama, Carl Malamud and Robert Richards also expressed interest and encouragement at an early stage. These sparks of recognition kept the fires of inspiration burning.

Legal and multilingual support in MLZ extend a second open-source project: the Citation Style Language (CSL). CSL is the brainchild of Bruce D'Arcus, who laid the foundations for its development years before it was given the breath of life by adoption in Zotero. Thanks to the effort of many contributors, CSL is something of a phenomenon in bibliographic circles. It has been (and continues to be) a pleasure to work with those who drive the project forward, including most especially Rintze Zelle (as CSL developer and release manager), and Sebastian Karcher (as prolific style author and CSL support guru).

The CSL formatter in MLZ (citeproc-js) is my own code, originally prepared for use in Zotero. The idea of writing a new formatter from scratch was prompted by preliminary JavaScript code shared by Erik Hetzner. It was pre-

ceded by Simon Kornblith's original CSL processor for Zotero, and by Andrea
Rossato's excellent citeproc-hs written in Haskell. Both Simon and Andrea generously provided advice based on their own deeper experience in development.
More recently, the project has been informed by feedback from Charles Parnot
(of Papers), Sylvester Keil (author of citeproc-ruby) and Simon Hewitt (of Docear).

Hints along the way were taken from experimental work in Python by Jo-
han Kool and Bruce D'Arcus. Detailed technical advice and hands-on feedback
from less-than-perfect releases of MLZ and citeproc-js has been received from
Faolan Cheslack-Postava, Fergus Gallagher, Simon Hewitt, James Jardine, Simon Kornblith, David Lester, Phillip Lord, Avram Lyon, Carles Pina, Mikko
Rönkkö and Aurimas Vinckevicius, among others.

Improvements to multilingual support were encouraged by generous support
from the Cluster of Excellence "Asia and Europe in a Global Context", of the
Karl Jaspers Centre for Advanced Transcultural Studies in Heidelberg University.

Invaluable feedback has been received from early adopters, many faced with
projects of significant size. Particular thanks are due to Rudolf Ammann, Hiro
Aragaki, Anna Clawson, Grégoire Colly, Eric Decker, Gonçalo Gato, Andrea
Hacker, Sras Hem, Nathan Hopson, Valdemaras Klumbys, Nop Kanharith, Won
Bok Lee, Peter Martin, Mariana Münning, Maxim Nazarenko, Jens Østergaard
Peterson, Phan Cong Thanh, Nicolas Pinet, Tiziana Scarramuzza, Stephan De
Spiegeleire, Sean Takats, Paul Troop, Ty Vichet, John Willinsky, Deborah M.
Weiss, and Olga Zelinska.

The legal styles documented in this volume are a collaborative product. Julia
Caldwell is the creator, with John Prebble, of the MLZ New Zealand Law style;
the MLZ McGill Guide styles are based on original work by Phillipe Tousignant
(French) and Liam McHugh-Russell (English); Sandra Meredith responded to
frequent questions during preparation of the MLZ OSCOLA style; and the foundation of MLZ Chicago Full Note is the original CSL style by Elena Razlogova.

My colleagues at Nagoya University opened the door to this project through
exceptional forbearance and patience that I gratefully acknowledge. Claudia
Ishikawa, Sean McGinty (who provided feedback on Chapter 1), Yoshiharu
Matsuura, Manabu Matsunaka, Yasutomo Morigiwa, and Saori Okuda deserve
special mention for their supportive interest.

Rintze Zelle generously reviewed a rough manuscript through several revisions, greatly improving its clarity and accuracy. Titus Nemeth provided the
artwork that graces the finished volume, after an initial cover design drew tactful
reservations from friends. I am much in debt for these acts of kindness.

My siblings have tolerated unacceptably long gaps in correspondence during this effort. I deeply regret being unable to present the completed work to our
mother, who passed away as the manuscript moved toward publication. Credit
for finally getting the project to press belongs to my spouse Mieko, whose pa-
tient resolve and gentle encouragement in the face of perennial declarations of
near-completion have well exceeded the ordinary bounds of human endurance.

Chapter 1

Introduction

I can see the dancin'
The silhouettes on the shade
I hear the music, all the lovers on parade
Open up, I wanna come in again
I thought you were my friend

—Yvonne Baker and the Sensations[1]

About this Book

This book is a coming-of-age celebration for Multilingual Zotero (MLZ), software that offers an alternative to the time-honoured practice of hand-crafting citations in legal and multilingual publishing. The long-term aim of the project is to improve the quality of our research lives by allowing us, as a community, to spend less time assembling documents and more time thinking about what should go into them.

The concept is simple and, as this Introduction explains in some detail, not particularly new. Reference management software has been around for a long time: but among the many products in circulation, none has yet offered robust support for legal or multilingual research. For a comparative lawyer with terrible handwriting and a mechanic's bent for computer programming, the temptation to meddle has proven too strong to resist.

The drive to build MLZ has been informed by the needs of international students in the faculty where I hold my appointment. The Nagoya University law programs are a microcosm of "globalisation", representing ten or more language domains in any given academic term. American lawyers are wont to protest, perhaps too much, at the burden of the "uniform" American legal citation system;[2] but researchers in the wider world face the harder task of navigating sources in

---

[1] THE SENSATIONS, LET ME IN (Chess Records 1961), *available at* http://www.youtube.com/watch?v=ef1znNdZA1k.

[2] *Compare* James D. Gordon, *How Not to Succeed in Law School*, 100 YALE L.J. 1679, 1692 (1991) ("The worst part of legal writing is having to learn the legal citation system. This is set forth in literally thousands of subrules in a book whose name nobody can remember, but which everybody calls the Bluebook, mostly because it's blue...."), *with* C.M. Bast & S. Harrell, *Has the Bluebook Met Its Match? The ALWD Citation Manual*, 92 LAW LIBR. J. 337, ¶ 6 (2000) ("[K]nowledge of correct legal citation distinguishes those who have legal education from those who do not.").

multiple languages, from a mixture of jurisdictions. The arcana of citation conventions in any one country pale against the demands of comparative research.

If these tasks can be simplified, the method for doing so can and should be shared. In the interest of broad dissemination, both the MLZ software and this text are freely available.[3] If you have already purchased a copy of the book, your money has not been wasted: sales of the volume help to assure the continued health of the MLZ project. If you are reading the freely distributed PDF version of this text and find that MLZ is useful in your work, please consider making that purchase. The version for sale has an elegant cover, and if we should one day meet, I will be happy to sign your copy in my terrible handwriting.

To introduce the software itself, a full MLZ installation is made up of three plugins for the Firefox browser:[4]

MLZ Client: This provides the same core facilities as Zotero proper, but with extensions to permit the attachment of supplementary translations and transliterations to individual metadata fields. The MLZ Client allows selective inclusion of this multilingual field content in generated citations.

Abbreviation Filter: This support plugin allows abbreviations to be applied to citation elements on a per-style basis. This is particularly useful for the proper implementation of legal citation styles.

Word Processor Plugins: The word processor plugins—the same as those developed for use with official Zotero—provide on-the-fly citation support for LibreOffice Writer, Word for Windows, and Word for Mac.

The remainder of this Introduction explains where MLZ comes from, why it has arrived so late on the scene, and how it fits into its surroundings as an open source, third-party product. Impatient readers may wish to skip forward to the *Getting Started* chapter, which covers the essential steps for installing and running the software.

The next section of this chapter reviews some of the more demanding requirements of legal and multilingual authoring, with brief notes on how MLZ handles each. The section can be used as a self-test questionnaire: if the citation issues described there look familiar, you are squarely within the target audience of the project; if not, other reference managers may suit your needs as well.

---

[3]See http://citationstylist.org/public/mlzbook.pdf

[4]Available via http://citationstylist.org/tools. Note that while MLZ is closely related to official Zotero at the code level, the two are separate projects. For clarity, MLZ should be referred to by that name when seeking support, and not by the name "Zotero". There are important differences between the two systems, and accurately identifying the software in use will yield a quicker, more accurate response to queries.

Hard Cases

To be concrete, there are five particularly challenging use cases that a reference manager with multilingual and legal support must address. These are reviewed here, with notes on how MLZ handles each using its extended variant of the Citation Style Language (referred to in this text as CSL-M).

(1) Multilingual: supplementary details

When citing resources outside the primary language of the document, adjustments to the content may be needed to make the reference accessible to the target audience. The most common case is transliteration. In a publication aimed at an English-speaking audience, for example, a reprint of the Japanese novel 坊っちゃん (bō chan) might be cited as follows:

> Natsume Sōseki, *Botchan* (Modernised edition, Shinchōsha 2003)

Transliterated titles may not be deemed sufficient. It may be desireable to add a translation, set off with distinctive punctuation:

> Natsume Sōseki, *Botchan* [The Little Master] (Modernised edition, Shinchōsha 2003)

Author names from some language domains may be difficult to distinguish in their romanised form. A recent trend in scientific publishing is to include author names in their original script in parentheses, resulting in a citation like the following:

> Natsume Sōseki (夏目漱石), *Botchan* [The Little Master] (Modernised edition, Shinchōsha 2003)

Some publishers ask that transliterated titles be forced to italics in citation forms that would otherwise use plain roman type. Compare the following newspaper reference:

> '*Yūsen shakuchi ken o minaoshi e: hisaichi taishō, haishi o kentō*' [Reconsideration of preferential lease rights: abolition in disaster relief zones under review], Asahi Shinbun (1 August 2012)

with

> Matthew L Wald, 'Court Weighs an Order on Yucca Mountain', New York Times (3 August 2012)

In our own faculty, providing the original script for both author and title is preferred:

> Natsume Sōseki (夏目漱石), *The Little Master* (坊っちゃん) (Modernised edition, Shinchōsha 2003)

In some environments one might wish to reverse the position of the original text:

> 夏目漱石 (Natsume Sōseki), 坊っちゃん [The Little Master] (Modernised edition, Shinchōsha 2003)

There are two problems to be solved: storing supplementary details (transliterations, translations) in the bibliographic record; and incorporating them into citations in a controlled way. MLZ supports alternative field values in any language or script, and a language preference panel permits multilingual data to be folded smoothly into finished citations. With MLZ, any of the 800+ official CSL styles can be used without modification in a multilingual context. (For details, see pages 25 to 27 below).

(2) Multilingual: style by language

Citation style conventions vary across language domains. For example, "title case" is a property of English-language citations:

> Edmund Curll, *A Complete Key to The Tale of a Tub; with Some Account of the Authors, the Occasion and Design of Writing It, and Mr. Wotton's Remarks Examin'd* (London, 1710)

but in French, title case is not used:

> René Macé and Giovanni Bocace (trs), *Les trois justaucorps, conte bleu, tiré de l'anglois du Révérend Mr Jonathan Swif [sic]* (Dublin, 1721)

More demanding adjustments may be needed when publishing for a polyglot readership, or where the local citation format has quite specialised requirements. In such environments it is common to cite foreign materials in a style appropriate to their own language domain. A translated work might be cited as follows in a Japanese context:

> Swift, Jonathan (著)、深町弘三(訳)「桶物語」190p 岩波文庫 1953.[5]

whereas the English original would be cited following Western conventions:

> Swift, Jonathan, *A Tale of a Tub* (London, J. Nutt 1704).

CSL-M allows entirely separate formats to be applied on a per-language basis using a standard language code, set in the Language field of the item (in these examples, en for English, fr for French, and ja for Japanese).

---

[5]This example is hand-crafted, as MLZ does not yet offer a Japanese citation style. The other examples in this section were generated using the MLZ OSCOLA style.

(3) Legal: style by jurisdiction

Even where document and citations are in the same language, citations to primary legal materials require distinctive formatting for particular jurisdictions. In the Oxford Standard for the Citation of Legal Authorities (OSCOLA), a case decided by a New York court might be cited as follows:

> *Palsgraf v Long Island Railway* 248 NY 339 (1928)

while a cite to a Canadian case would look like this:

> *Swiss Bank Corp v Air Canada* (1987) [1988] 1 FC 71 (CA)

Similarly, a specific form of citation might be used for documents issued by certain institutions:

> Universal Declaration of Human Rights, GA Res 217(III)A UN Doc A/RES/217(III)

Jurisdiction-specific adjustments to citation form are unavoidable in the law, and like language discrimi-

nation, they require a hint in the item data. In MLZ, legal item types have a Jurisdiction field that sets this value from a controlled list.

(4) Legal: meaningful fragments

In a reference manager, the basic unit of content is the *item*. In most cases, the item is naturally taken to be the entire work cited. An example in the American Law style:

> (1) DAVID LODGE, SMALL WORLD 23 (Penguin Books 1995).
>
> (2) *Id.* at 97.

The first reference above is to page 23 of *Small World*; the second is to page 97 of the same novel. Following the requirements of the style, the citation details of the second reference are replaced with *id.* The American Law style applies the same logic to statutes:

> (3) 33 USC § 3841(a).
>
> (4) *Id.* § 3802(b).

The citation pairs above look similar, but they refer to very different resources. The novel (like most forms of writing) does not have a rigid internal structure amenable to consistent referencing. Narrative works can be divided in various ways, and pagination varies across editions. The narrative text as a whole is the most reliable point of reference, for *both* citation *and* record-keeping purposes.

Statutes, on the other hand, are divided into discrete provisions at the point of publication, each of which may be the focus of detailed interpretation and debate. In note-taking, these are often a more natural unit of reference than the statute as a whole. Accordingly, MLZ permits single pro-

visions to be recorded in the database, by setting the pinpoint information in the Section field, as shown in the illustration. (For details, see page 34 below; for examples, see pages 78, 80 and 81 below.)

(5) Legal: parallel citations

Court judgments in certain jurisdictions may be published in multiple reports. Some citation systems require that these reports be cited in parallel:

> Hanna v. Plumer, 380 US 460, 461, 85 S. Ct. 1136, 1137 (1965).[6]

In MLZ, each report of a case is stored as an individual item. It is up to the author to cite them in the appropriate order; but as the example above shows, the citation formatter will take over from there, producing a "collapsed" parallel citation that begins with the title common to the items in the set, and ends with common trailing matter (in this case, the date).

The MLZ citation engine will also handle parallel citations to statutory law and treaties:

> White Slave Traffic (Mann) Act, ch. 395, 36 Stat. 825, 826 (1910).
>
> National Environmental Policy Act of 1969, § 102, 42 USC § 4332 (1969).
>
> Department of Transportation Act, Pub. L. No. 89-670, § 9, 80 Stat. 931, 931 (1966).
>
> Treaty of Friendship, Commerce and Navigation, United States-Japan, art. X, 4 U.S.T. 2063, 75 U.N.T.S. 135.

Here as well, if the items are cited in the appropriate order, the formatter will produce a correct parallel citation.

Software and Science

Scientists were quick to harness information technology in support of the writing process. Document processing software with automated bibliography sup-

---

[6]In this example, the numbers 461 and 1137 are pinpoint page references, indicating the exact page on which the statement supporting the author's argument appears.

port first emerged from computer science faculties in the 1970s.[7] The principle surviving representative of this initial wave of innovation is the open-licensed LaTeX/BibTeX document system. Reference managers for use with WYSIWYG word processors and personal computers made their debut in the 1980s, in a second wave of development. The leading example of these today is the proprietary EndNote product.[8] The utility of these tools is reflected in the extent of their deployment, with LaTeX boasting a broad base of users in maths-intensive disciplines, and EndNote claiming an installed base in the millions.[9]

These early projects were aimed at different audiences. LaTeX was built to serve the scientific community, where computing skills are plentiful. EndNote (like other members of the second wave) is aimed at a broader audience who may be familiar with word processors, but less adept at programming. The respective licensing terms of LaTeX and EndNote reflect this difference. Where the user community is well-equipped to make significant contributions to a software product, open code is attractive; but where the community is less able to contribute, the revenue stream from proprietary distribution offers a more certain path to sustainability. Both models obviously work; which works best depends on the makeup of the user community.

Neither of the early waves has produced a general solution for legal or multilingual referencing. In part this has simply been a matter of timing. The early gains from information technology in the legal sphere involved the publication of large volumes of data. Given the high cost of entry, expertise was initially concentrated in a few commercial ventures, and the incentives to invest in automated referencing and other marginal improvements were rather thin.[10] As for multilingual support, innovation depends in the first instance on standards that simply did not exist in 1980.[11] Multilingual capabilities have been added to

---

[7]*See e.g.* BRIAN K. REID, SCRIBE: INTRODUCTORY USER'S MANUAL (Computer Science Department, Carnegie-Mellon University 1978); LESLIE LAMPORT, LaTeX: A DOCUMENT PREPARATION SYSTEM (1985) (documenting the companion BibTeX bibliography management system by Oren Patashnik).

[8]*See e.g.* Ruth E. Wachtel, *Personal Bibliographic Databases*, 235 SCI. 1093 (New Series, 1987) (reviewing five offerings: Reference Manager, Scholar's Bibliofile, Ref-11, Pro-Cite, and Sci-Mate); *Oral History of Ernest Beutler*, LEGENDS IN HEMATOLOGY (American Society of Hematology Nov. 6, 1990), http://www.hematology.org/Publications/Legends/Beutler/1599.aspx (placing the first release of Reference Manager in mid-1984); About Niles & Associates, Inc. (Nov. 12, 1996), http://web.archive.org/web/19961112110744/http://www.niles.com/home/Company.htm (indicating that the first version of the EndNote program was written in 1985); *also* Personal email from Victor Rosenberg, (no subject) (Jun. 14, 2012) (indicating that Pro-Cite was developed at University of Michigan, licensed to a commercial firm in 1982, and first marketed in July 1983).

[9]*EndNote*, THOMSON REUTERS: PRODUCTS A-Z, http://thomsonreuters.com/products_services/science/science_products/a-z/endnote/.

[10]See discussion *infra* at pages 8 to 17.

[11]The design of Unicode was proposed in 1988, and the Unicode Consortium that serves as caretaker of the standard was launched in 1991. Joseph D. Becker, Unicode 88 (1988); *Chronology of Unicode Version 1.0*, THE UNICODE CONSORTIUM, http://www.unicode.org/history/versionone.html.

the early products over time,[12] but support for multilingual authoring in legacy products remains awkward and incomplete.

The "third wave" in reference management, of which MLZ is a member, is being fueled by changes in the target audience—that is to say, ourselves, the general community of researchers. Programming skills are more broadly distributed today. Powerful high-level languages and toolsets allow more work to be done with less code. Collaborative software development tools are more advanced and more accessible, and even multilingual text processing is now simpler and more standardised.[13] These changes have enabled the development of Zotero and others (colwiz, Docear, Mendeley, pandoc, Papers, Qiqqa). In today's environment, detailed feedback and code contributions by a proportion of users is more common, and this goes a long way toward explaining why Zotero, a flagship of the "third wave", is distributed and maintained as free and open software.[14]

Open digital infrastructure for legal and multilingual research is relatively young, but it is evolving rapidly. With low costs of dissemination, projects draw feedback and contributions from a broadly dispersed target audience at an early stage. Tools built on an open-source model offer the assurance of availability over the long term, an important attraction for professional researchers. Finally, in the legal sphere in particular, open architectures have a significant role to play in promoting standards-based development and innovation.

Law and Order

Legal resources have particularly demanding citation requirements, and to some extent this is unavoidable. Legal citation styles and legal research software must strike a balance between simplicity and the demands of the field, while taking care to prevent complexity from running out of control.

Legislation and administrative rules are subject to revision and recompilation. A target text may be an *original act* creating entirely new law, an *amending act* specifying only the changes to be made to existing law, or a *consolidated act* in which changes are merged into a finished revised text. Finally, current acts (original or consolidated) may be reorganised for inclusion in a *codification scheme* such as the U.S. Code or the Code of Federal Regulations. Citations in legal argument must identify the exact text relied upon; and because rulemaking

---

[12] *See* Donald E. Knuth, *The New Versions of TEX and Metafont*, 10 TUGBOAT 325 (1989) (introducing TEX 3.0, with support for 256 character sets); Oren Patashnik, *BibTEX Yesterday, Today, and Tomorrow*, 24 TUGBOAT 25, (listing m (Proceedings of the 2003 Annual Meeting, 2003) ultilingual support as a goal for the next phase of BibTEX development).

[13] *See supra* note 11.

[14] The citeproc-js citation formatting engine written by the author is distributed under alternative free software licenses (AGPL and CPAL), and runs in the core of Mendeley, Qiqqa, Zotero, and other projects in the third wave. Styles in the official CSL repository are distributed under a Creative Commons BY-SA license. Both Zotero itself and the MLZ system introduced by this book are distributed under an AGPL license.

processes vary across jurisdictions, citation methods must do so as well. Hence some degree of complexity, not to say arbitrariness, is inevitable.

On the other hand, *judicial judgments* seem at first blush to be less daunting. A legal ruling is an immutable document, issued by a decision-making body at a single point in time. In terms of citation, such material appears to differ little from a journal article: given a canonical document, all that would seem to be required is a uniform scheme for describing it. The significance of a judgment is heavily dependent on context, however. Decisions may be subject to appeal, and while an appellate judgment is also a single immutable text, the procedural history of a given legal case is essential to understanding the significance of the individual steps contributing to the final result. In addition, the rule or interpretation expressed in a final judgment may be modified or overturned by entirely separate judgments in other cases at a later point in time. Legal citation systems, and reference managers that aim to automate them, need to reflect some of this detail, and that inevitably adds to their complexity.

The wrinkles described above are inherent features of the law itself. Further complications arise from the ways in which legal text is published. Once issued by the court, a legal judgment may be disseminated through multiple channels, some of which may be more readily accessible to some readers. Accordingly, many legal styles in the U.S. (and certain other jurisdictions) require that parallel references be provided when a judgment is available through multiple reporters or services. Such citations typically have special formatting requirements, omitting some elements of each cite in the series of parallels to save space and improve readability. For example:[15]

> Harvard Crimson, Inc. v. President and Fellows of Harvard Coll. 445 Mass. 745, 840 N.E.2d 518 (2006).

Legal citation styles are thus complex things, in part because of the difficulty of the underlying material and in part due to idiosyncrasies of the publishing chain (factors aggravated, as we have seen, by variation across the world's legal systems).

Compleat rules of citation

The leading U.S. legal style began life as a short pamphlet entitled "A Uniform System of Citation: Abbreviations and Form of Citation", prepared in 1926 by future Dean Erwin Griswold while a member of the Harvard Law Review.[16]

The more relaxed atmosphere of legal publishing in those halcyon days is captured by the tone of this modest document of 26 pages, prefaced as it is by

---

[15] In civil law jurisdictions where extra-judicial commentary plays an important role in legal interpretation, case notes and the like may be appended to a case reference in a similar shorthand fashion.

[16] *See* Darby Dickerson, *An Un-uniform System of Citation: Surviving with the New Bluebook*, 26 STETSON L. REV. 53, 57 (1996); James W. Paulsen, *An Uninformed System of Citation*, 105 HARV. L. REV. 1780, 1782 (1992).

the following disclaimer, destined to remain substantially unchanged through nine subsequent editions over a period of forty years:

> *This pamphlet does not pretend to include a complete list of abbreviations or all the necessary data as to form. It aims to deal with the more common abbreviations and forms to which one has occasion to refer.* (Bluebook 1926)[17]

Such were the humble seeds of hegemonic ambition. The pamphlet became a "booklet" in 1934, having grown to some 48 pages. Two years later, it was printed with a copyright notice for the first time, with the names of three other leading law reviews listed as joint proprietors. At the first national conference of law review editors, held in 1949, the style was the sole candidate put forward as a national form of citation.[18] Beginning with the eleventh edition (published, coincidentally, in the year of Dean Griswold's retirement), the tone of the guide began to take on a more assertive quality, dropping the declaration of incompleteness, and offering the following stern observation:

> *The editors are unable to recommend that the Third Edition* Merriam-Webster New International Dictionary *replace the Second Edition as a general authority for definition and italicization. The new edition fails to distinguish those foreign words which should be italicised in English writing, and is in general insufficiently prescriptive.*
> (Bluebook 1967)[19] (underlining added)

From that point forward, the guide has progressively expanded in scope and detail to become the 511-page monolith that graces the desks of lawyers today. A disenchanted readership has responded by treating each fresh edition to a small eddy of satirical review.[20]

There have been two attempts to launch competing projects. The Chicago Manual of Legal Citation (the "Maroonbook") debuted in 1986, aiming for a simpler set of guidelines supplemented by common sense and convention.[21] The first edition of the ALWD Citation Manual was published in 2000 by Darby

---

[17] A UNIFORM SYSTEM OF CITATION 1 (1926).

[18] Paulsen, *supra* note 16, at 1783.

[19] A UNIFORM SYSTEM OF CITATION, at ii (11th ed. 1967).

[20] *See, e.g.* Richard A. Posner, *Goodbye to the Bluebook*, 53 U. CHI. L. REV. 1343, 1343–44 (1986) ("The particular faults of the Bluebook ... place it in the mainstream of American legal thought. ... The vacuity and tendentiousness of so much legal reasoning are concealed by the awesome scrupulousness with which a set of intricate rules governing the form of citations is observed."); Alan Strasser, *Technical Due Process?*, HARV. C.R.-C.L L. REV. 507 (1977) ("[The Bluebook's rules of citation] increase the speed at which the legal enterprise slows down."); *and* Jim C. Chen, *Something Old, Something New, Something Borrowed, Something Blue*, 58 U. CHI. L. REV. 1527, 1528 (1991) ("For those who think too intensely about law—including anyone who ever edited or wrote a law review article—the Bluebook serves as a morality play too dull to endure but too conspicuous to ignore.").

[21] *See* Posner, *Goodbye to the Bluebook*, *supra* note 20.

Dickerson and the Association of Legal Writing Directors. In contrast to the Maroonbook, the ALWD Manual largely sought to replicate the rules of the leading guide, but with better presentation and attention to consistency.[22] Neither of these projects has come close to usurping the leading guide, although both are now well established in their respective niches. Of the two, the ALWD Manual is thought to have enjoyed the larger take-up.[23]

Seeking to explain the staying power of the unpopular incumbent, one reviewer has looked to network effects—the economic theory that users as a class may adhere to a standard product for its value to them as a community, despite the availability of technically superior, less widely adopted alternatives.[24] Following this logic, the market for citation styles may to some degree be "path-dependent".[25]

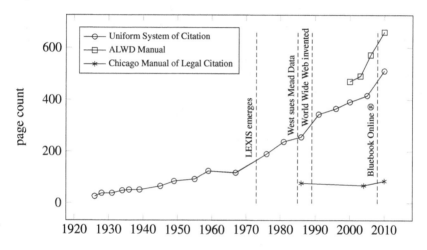

Figure 1.1: U.S. legal style guides and information technology

Unfortunately, the path in this case is pretty clearly headed over a cliff. Figure 1.1 shows the page counts of the leading style and its would-be competitors as a function of time. While the Maroonbook has striven for compactness,[26] the more "compatible" ALWD Manual has tracked the inflationary tendency of the leading guide. If this confirms the expectations of network effects theory, that would hardly be a cause for celebration, since the primary complaint directed at the leading style is its sheer bulk.

---

[22] *See* Bast & Harrell, *supra* note 2.

[23] *See, e.g.* Christine Hurt, *Network Effects and Legal Citation*, 87 Iowa L. Rev. 1257, 1281 (2002). Adoptions of the ALWD Citation Manual can be viewed online at http://www.alwd.org/publications/adoptions.html.

[24] *Id.* at 1284–85; Joseph Farrell & Garth Saloner, *Standardization, Compatibility, and Innovation*, 16 RAND J. Econ. 70 (1985).

[25] Hurt, *supra* note 23.

[26] Posner, *Goodbye to the Bluebook, supra* note 20.

There is bittersweet irony in the fact that the lawyerly burden of typing things correctly began escalating with the arrival of information technology. Unfortunately, this correlation is not a coincidence. To paraphrase Pogo, the legal profession has met the enemy, and he is us.[27]

The public launch of the LEXIS service by Mead Data Central in 1973 (flagged in Figure 1.1) marked the arrival of electronic search and retrieval systems as a tool for legal research. This posed a challenge to West Publishing Company, the dominant legal publisher in the U.S., with its comprehensive range of (print-published) case reports.[28] West responded by introducing its own electronic service in 1975.[29] Ten years later LEXIS, by then a comprehensive service in its own right, announced a plan for "star pagination"—markup in electronic text indicating page boundaries in the West case reports. West resorted to law, suing on the grounds that its page numbers were protected by copyright. After a judgment in favour of West was upheld by the Eight Circuit Court of Appeals[30] the parties settled,[31] reputedly for a relatively modest payment of $50,000 per year.[32] West continued to assert copyright in its page numbering against other vendors[33] until 1998, when the Court of Appeals for the Second Circuit upheld a district court judgment that such details are "insubstantial, unoriginal, and uncreative" and not subject to copyright protection.[34]

Today, the U.S. legal system is heavily reliant on electronic text retrieval and associated systems. These services have real value because of their scope, speed and accuracy, extending the lawyer's access to the raw stuff of legal research. The market has been crucial to their development, but market incentives can cut both ways: when they undercut the openness on which innovation depends, they can become an impediment.

A market for consistency

In modern electronic library systems, documents can be retrieved in one of three ways. The most familiar to readers will be the URL, a specially formatted string first defined by Tim Berners-Lee while working at the CERN research institute

---

[27] THE BEST OF POGO 224 (Mrs. Walt Kelly & Bill Crouch Jr. eds., 1982).

[28] *See* Robert M. Jarvis, *John B. West*, 50 AM. J. LEGAL HIST. 1 (2008).

[29] *See* James A. Sprowl, *The Westlaw System: A Different Approach to Computer-Assisted Legal Research*, 16 JURIMETRICS J. 142 (1975).

[30] West Publishing Co. v. Mead Data Center, Inc., 616 F. Supp. 1571 (D. Minn. 1985), aff'd, 799 F.2d 1219 (8th Cir. 1986), cert. denied, 479 U.S. 1070 (1986).

[31] *West, Mead Settle Lawsuits Over Computerized Legal Research Market*, AP NEWS ARCHIVE (Jul. 21, 1988), http://www.apnewsarchive.com/1988/West-Mead-Settle-Lawsuits-Over-Computerized-Legal-Research-Market/id-d5b6fc6cf1202c42e5f85454a664a380.

[32] *See* WIKIPEDIA *Westlaw* (2013), http://en.wikipedia.org/wiki/Westlaw.

[33] Matthew Bender & HyperLaw v. West, 94 Civ. 0589 (S.D.N.Y. 1996) (citing "testimony by various West employees in which they state that they do not know of any companies that have used West's star pagination that West has not sued").

[34] Matthew Bender & Hyperlaw v. West, 158 F.3d 674, ¶ 41 (2d Cir. 1998).

in 1989.[35] As everyone reading this is *well* aware, a URL looks something like
this:

```
http://digitalcommons.law.yale.edu/fss_papers/498/
```

URLs can be unsightly and awkward to manage. They are also tied to a
single copy of the document, which may become unavailable. To provide a
more robust means of tracking down documents, unique identifiers have been
developed that can be assigned to a published work independent of its location.
Typical examples are PMID[36] (for medicine and the life sciences), DOI[37] (for
digital materials generally) and ISBN[38] (for books). Such identifiers form part
of the *metadata* describing the work. On the World Wide Web, identifiers can be
submitted to a special website (a "resolver") to obtain more complete metadata
(perhaps including a URL that leads to the target resource itself). A DOI, to take
one example, might look something like this:

```
10.1111/j.1747-4469.1976.tb00951.x
```

By dropping the text of this identifier into a resolver or a search engine, we can
obtain a set of links to the article in the preceding example.

Unique identifiers are a relatively recent innovation, and not all articles
and books have them. Even if they do, they might not be known to the researcher—for example, the DOI above is not recited in the text of the article
itself. In such cases, *structured metadata* that describes the resource can also be
used to find it via a resolver, in effect automating the process of looking up the
work in a library card catalog or the like.

Structured metadata can take many forms, but a couple of examples will
suffice to illustrate the concept. In the BibTeX format, metadata for the article
associated with the DOI above looks like this:

```
@article{langbein_market_1976,
    title = {Market Funds and {Trust-Investment} Law},
    volume = {1},
    issn = {0361-9486},
    url = {http://www.jstor.org/stable/827950},
    number = {1},
    journal = {American Bar Foundation Research Journal},
    author = {Langbein, John H. and Posner, Richard A.},
    month = jan,
    year = {1976},
    pages = {1--34}
}
```

---

[35] Tim Berners-Lee, Information Management: A Proposal (CERN 1989).

[36] *See* National Center for Biotechnology Information, *Search Field Descriptions and Tags*,
PUBMED HELP (2005), http://www.ncbi.nlm.nih.gov/books/NBK3830/.

[37] *See* International DOI Foundation, *Overviews and Standards*, THE DOI SYSTEM, http://www
.doi.org/about_the_doi.html.

[38] *See* International ISBN Agency FAQs, http://www.isbn-international.org/faqs.

In the RIS format, a description of the same article would look something like this:

```
TY  -  JOUR
ID  -  8052
T1  -  Market Funds and Trust-Investment Law
JF  -  American Bar Foundation Research Journal
A1  -  Langbein,John H.
A1  -  Posner,Richard A.
VL  -  1
IS  -  1
PY  -  1976/01/01/
SP  -  1
EP  -  34
SN  -  0361-9486
UR  -  http://www.jstor.org/stable/827950
ER  -
```

Technologists can grow quite agitated about the details of metadata formats, but for our purposes the key point is simply that structured metadata *is structured*, so that computers can parse out the content and do interesting and useful things with it. Using either of the structured descriptions above, a computer can retrieve a list of other works by the authors, reconstruct the table of contents of the journal issue in which their article appears, or search for other articles in which it is cited. Accurate, rich and plentiful metadata is the lifeblood of modern information systems. It makes them smart, responsive, and unintrusive.

While citations and metadata share the same general purpose, they have distinct roles, and the difference is easy to miss. In a review of the nineteenth edition of the Bluebook, Richard Posner contrasts the leading style guide with a simpler, less prescriptive stylesheet used by clerks in his chambers.[39] In a (sympathetic) column published in response, Stephen and Jonathan Darrow question the wisdom of diverging too sharply from the conventions of the leading style:[40]

> *Although Westlaw properly processed most of Posner's Bluebook-defying citation forms, it choked on some seemingly reasonable abbreviations that we postulated. For example, abbreviating the word "Technology" as "Tech." in "13 Albany Law Journal of Science and Tech. 751" resulted in a Westlaw error message.*

A researcher in a field other than law might well ask, "Why on earth does this matter?" After all, citations exist for the convenience of people. For the convenience of computers, we have structured metadata and unique identifiers. The problem (and the reason the point made by Darrow and Darrow is valid as far as it goes) is that we *don't have* structured metadata or unique identifiers for

---

[39] Richard A. Posner, *The Bluebook Blues*, 120 YALE L.J. 850, 853 (2011).

[40] Stephen M. Darrow & Jonathan J. Darrow, *Beating the Bluebook Blues: a Response to Judge Posner*, 109 MICH. L. REV. FIRST IMPRESSIONS 92, 95 (2011).

U.S. legal materials. If we are most lawyers, we probably don't even know what they are.

Despite the extraordinarily demanding citation requirements of the U.S. jurisdiction, American lawyers are seldom exposed to metadata in a structured form. The article referenced in the examples above is available in the popular Westlaw legal research service (once we have overcome the "Westlaw error message"), but in contrast to aggregator services in other fields,[41] Westlaw provides only the text of the article, with no structured metadata. The same is true of most content offered by the leading legal information services in the U.S. market: no DOIs or other unique identifiers; no structured metadata.

As stated in their literature, Westlaw, Lexis, and other aggregators of U.S. case law aim to provide comprehensive research support.[42] Such services depend internally on unique identifiers and fine-grained metadata of the kind described above, but that data is not exposed; at the customer level, the only identifier shared in common between Westlaw, Lexis and other services is the one we were using back in 1926:[43] the properly formatted citation, in the leading style, as it would appear on the printed page.

The escalating page counts shown in Figure 1.1 are thus the end result of forcing citations (intended for humans) to serve as machine-readable metadata. Achieving uniformity by dint of an instruction manual is possible, but it requires a *very long* instruction manual. That, plus a lot of patience or a lot of paid help.

Consistency alone is not quite enough to make citations serve (approximately) as document identifiers. Some mechanism must enable machines to identify and interpret human-readable citations within a document, so that they can be resolved to proper identifiers and, ultimately, addresses. For better or for worse, such a mechanism does exist, in the form of *regular expression* pattern-matching, a common feature of all major scripting and programming languages.[44] Regular expressions look something like this:

```
/L=\|(?<volume>\d+)?\s?U\.\s?S\.\s?(?<page>\d+)
\s*?\|>(?<anchored>\d+)/
```

If it is not clear what this example does, that itself would be the point precisely. Regular expressions are opaque, complex, prone to error and difficult to debug. This is compounded by the fact that different tools interpret this slippery code in different ways.[45]

---

[41] A welcome oasis in the American legal metadata desert is HeinOnline, the leading aggregator of law review content offered by William S. Hein & Co.

[42] *See, e.g.* Thomson Reuters, *Research fundamentals: getting started with online research*, WESTLAW 1 (Jun. 2010), http://lscontent.westlaw.com/images/content/GettingStarted10.pdf ("The Westlaw legal research service is comprehensive, easy to use, and up-to-date. It will help you perform accurate and effective legal research.").

[43] *See* Posner, *The Bluebook Blues*, *supra* note 39, at 857, *citing* Paulsen, *supra* note 16, at 1782–85.

[44] *See generally* JEFFREY E.F. FRIEDL, MASTERING REGULAR EXPRESSIONS (3d ed. 2006).

[45] Donald Knuth once remarked, "I define UNIX as 30 definitions of regular expressions living under one roof." DONALD E. KNUTH, DIGITAL TYPOGRAPHY 649 (1998).

In the words of Jamie Zawinski, lead developer for the Netscape browser:

> *Some people, when confronted with a problem, think 'I know, I'll use regular expressions.'*
>
> *Now they have two problems.*[46]

Widespread reliance on human-readable citations in contexts that call for proper structured metadata is poor design. Systems that rely heavily on such code can be expected to break from time to time, and legal information systems in the metadata-starved U.S. jurisdiction tend to do just that.

Legal publishing is not *entirely* starved of metadata, and the benefits are readily apparent where it does exist. The *Albany Law Journal of Science and Technology* article tested by Darrow and Darrow is served with structured metadata by HeinOnline[47] (in the COinS format). When visiting the article's page there, Zotero or MLZ can leverage this data in several ways. We can:

- Add an item for the article to our Zotero or MLZ database;

- Find copies of the article supplied by other vendors;

- Attach a copy of the article to the Zotero or MLZ item just created;

- Insert a citation for the article into a document.

It is not necessary to laboriously type out citation details for these operations. That was done once by the maintainers of HeinOnline when the article was published, and there is no need to do it again. Systems based on structured metadata just work.

Electronic library systems require unique, uniform identifiers for machine-driven referencing. In the U.S. jurisdiction, and in many others, citations originally written for people serve this purpose. We impose rigid rules on their construction—to an extent that interferes with other work—because a looser approach could cause the cross-referencing on which our fragile information infrastructure depends to completely fall apart.

In a normal market, the leading style would have plenty of competition. The Maroon Book, the ALWD guide, the McGill Guide or the OSCOLA guide, not to mention Judge Posner's brief stylesheet, are all perfectly worthy alternatives. There is far greater variety in citation style in other disciplines (admittedly there may be *too much* variety, but that is a separate conversation). Because they are rich in metadata, other disciplines have the freedom to choose how they want their cites to appear. In U.S. law, without publicly accessible metadata, we have not enjoyed that freedom.

---

[46]*See* Jeffrey E.F. Freidl, *Source of the famous "Now you have two problems" quote*, JEFFREY FRIEDL'S BLOG (Sep. 15, 2006), http://regex.info/blog/2006-09-15/247.

[47]William S. Hein, *List of Libraries*, HEINONLINE, http://home.heinonline.org/content/list-of-libraries/.

If legal citations play an "addressing" role similar to that of DOIs and URLs, the specification for creating them is managed in a very different way. The standards document that defines the format of URLs carries the following note concerning republication:

> *Distribution of this memo is unlimited.*[48]

Developing standards is neither easy nor cheap, but those underpinning the Web are distributed freely, to the extent that the major players see interoperability as good for business: when firms support collaborative standards processes, they do so out of self-interest. As we have seen, interoperability is not a priority amongst comprehensive content providers in the U.S. market. The gap has been filled by the leading style (as a workaround standard), maintained as in the past by a narrow circle of law students, and supported by sales of the manual in both printed and electronic form. Thus we find that the online version of the leading style is published with the following restriction:

> *Except as expressly provided by this Agreement, any use of the Site and its content is strictly prohibited without our written consent.*[49]

The uncommonly strong demand for uniformity in the U.S. jurisdiction has thus led to a pay-per-view model for funding legal style maintenance and development. This approach rewards expansion of the guide itself,[50] discourages moves toward proper automation, and appears to have reached a point of diminishing returns as far as users are concerned.

Moving Forward

Resource retrieval and citation formatting are related tasks, both of which can be automated; the real work for any writer lies between these steps. Like Zotero, MLZ can extract generic metadata from online resources, and store it in a consistent, structured form in a user database. Items not available online can be input manually.[51] Once stored locally, database items can be used to fashion correctly formatted citations in user documents. In be-

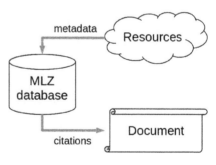

---

[48]Roy Fielding et al., Hypertext Transfer Protocol—HTTP/1.1, RFC 2616 (The Internet Society 1999).

[49]Harvard Law Review Ass'n, *Terms of Use*, THE BLUEBOOK (Feb. 15, 2008), https://www.legalbluebook.com/public/TermsOfUse.aspx.

[50]*See* Posner, *The Bluebook Blues, supra* note 39, at 852.

[51]Metadata field assignments are illustrated in the *Item Examples* appendix. See page 43 below.

tween research and writing, items stored in the database can be searched, tagged
and annotated as desired.

Citation forms and abbreviation
conventions vary between styles and
jurisdictions. In MLZ, abbreviations
are applied by the Abbreviation Filter, a Firefox plugin that provides a
conversion layer between the content
of the MLZ database and the formatting engine (citeproc-js) as shown to

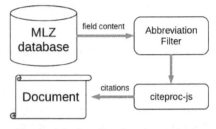

the right. Abbreviation lists are style-specific, and for legal styles, in particular,
the logic coded into the lists is necessary for proper formatting.

The remainder of this book concerns specifics of the MLZ system. Like any
complex software, the project is a moving target, and the current version may
differ in some details from the description provided here. Significant changes
introduced after the time of writing will be documented (together with errata) at
the following URL:

```
http://citationstylist.org/errata
```

The following two chapters, *Getting Started* and *Under the Bonnet*, offer
basic information on installing, operating and extending MLZ. The instructions
are not comprehensive; links to relevant resources on the Web are provided for
users who wish to dig deeper than the outline view supplied here. The Appendices provide guidance on the data entry patterns for particular types of content,
based on the fields available in MLZ and variables recognised in the extended
CSL-M version of the Citation Style Language.

Chapter 2

Getting Started

> *It's called Progenitorivox*
> *It's made by SquabbMerlCo*
> *It's a life enhancing miracle*
> *But there are some things you should know ...*
> —The Austin Lounge Lizards[52]

Getting Oriented

Setting up an MLZ system is straightforward: install Firefox and three Firefox plugins and you are done. MLZ is based on Zotero, and much of the documentation on the Zotero website (http://zotero.org) applies equally to the multilingual variant. The two systems are not identical, however, and there are indeed a few things you should know before proceeding. Here is a short list of items to bear in mind:

Citation Styles: Multilingual and legal citation styles for MLZ are written in CSL-M, an extension of the CSL language used by Zotero. The number of CSL-M styles is currently small, but if you do not need legal citation support, the styles in the Zotero Style Repository will also work with MLZ. (You can also create your own CSL-M styles, of course. For further details, see page 31 below.)

Database: Upon installation, MLZ will replace an existing copy of Zotero, and use the same database. This is a one-way operation, as MLZ makes database adjustments that are incompatible with official Zotero. (This affects the database only: it is possible to sync libraries to both the MLZ Client and to official Zotero. For further details, see page 32 below.)

Fields and Item Types: MLZ adds several item types and fields to those found in Zotero. The full set of MLZ fields is documented in the Appendices.[53] Many fields in MLZ can be supplemented by attaching transliterations or translations to them, for use in multilingual publishing environments.

[52]THE AUSTIN LOUNGE LIZARDS, *The Drugs I Need*, on THE DRUGS I NEED (Blue Corn Music 2006), *available at* http://www.youtube.com/watch?v=eZPZG92iYE4.

[53]For the differences, see http://fbennett.github.io/z2csl/diffMap.html.

Sync Behaviour: The Zotero Sync service, which MLZ also uses, recognises only the standard fields and item types of official Zotero. Additional fields and other data stored on MLZ items is inserted into the Extra field in a computer-friendly syntax (JSON format) when items are synced. The data is visible in this form in the Extra field when viewed in an MLZ library at zotero.org, but items will display normally when synced to a local MLZ Client library. (Note that the Extra field should not be edited in the online view. For further details see page 32 below.)

Installing Things

Sparks fly shootin' out
Makin' sure that everything is workin'

—The Talking Heads[54]

The three Firefox plugins making up an MLZ system are described below.[55] At the time of writing, MLZ is not available in a standalone version.

MLZ Client

If you already have Zotero installed, your first step should be to back up your existing database.[56] This will allow you to move back to official Zotero if necessary.

To install the MLZ Client, visit http://citationstylist.org in Firefox and click on the button shown to the right. Firefox will guide you

Install
Multilingual Zotero Client

through the installation process. If Zotero was previously installed, a message like that shown in Figure 2.1 will appear when Firefox restarts. Clicking Next to proceed will modify your database for use with MLZ. You can check that MLZ was successfully installed in Firefox by pressing Ctrl + Alt + Z (on Windows or Linux) or Shift + Cmd + Z (on Mac) to open the MLZ interface.

Abbreviation Filter

The Abbreviation Filter is available from the same page as the MLZ Client. Click on its Install button, follow the menus to restart Firefox, and the fil-

Install
Abbreviation Filter

---

[54] THE TALKING HEADS, *Facts of Life*, *on* NAKED (Sire 1988), *available at* http://www.youtube.com/watch?v=xee3cDQymE4.

[55] Firefox itself is available from: http://mozilla.org/firefox.

[56] For backup instructions see https://www.zotero.org/support/zotero_data.

ter will be ready for action. The Abbreviation Filter cannot be opened directly; it is accessible only through a Zotero word processor plugin, which is next on our list of things to install.

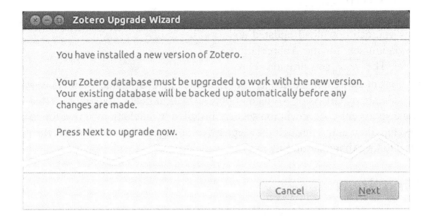

Figure 2.1: Upgrade warning for existing Zotero database

Word Processor Plugin

MLZ uses the same word processor plugins as official Zotero. On the Zotero website, click on the big red "Download Now" button, then click on the  link reading Add a plugin for Word or LibreOffice. Plugins are available for Word for Windows, Word for Mac, and LibreOffice Writer. Choose the plugin that fits your word processor, and follow the menus to finish the install.

After installing the plugin, restart Firefox and the word processor. In Word 2008 for Mac, the plugin but-  tons will appear in the "Word script menu", opened from an icon in the toolbar. In other versions of Word, it will be in the "Add-ins" toolbar. In LibreOffice Writer, the buttons should be visible in the Writer toolbar itself.

If you have difficulty getting word processor integration to work, check the Zotero documentation under http://zotero.org/support for troubleshooting tips; the plugins in MLZ work exactly as they do in Zotero, and the advice given there is a good starting point for working through any problems.

Styles and abbreviations

If you are using MLZ for legal writing, you can update the CSL-M styles by reinstalling them. These are available from the CitationStylist site, together with the MLZ Client and Abbreviation Filter.[57] Next to the description of each style, you will find a set of buttons such as those shown in the illustration below. Clicking on a [Style] button will install the relevant style (the same as in the Zotero Style Repository).

Using the [Abbr] and [Hints] buttons you can download updated abbreviation sets for the Abbreviation Filter. The [Abbr] sets provide abbre-

viations of entire fields (such as a journal title or a court name). The [Hints] sets provide abbreviations of words and phrases within fields, and are available for some styles only. Abbreviation sets are installed by clicking to save a file to the desktop, then going through the steps given at page 34 below to install the new set into the Abbreviation Filter.

First Steps

> *If you ever have to go to Shoeburyness*
> *Take the A road, the okay road that's the best*
> *Go motorin' on the A13*
>
> —Billy Bragg[58]

For experienced Zotero users and newcomers to reference management software alike, early familiarity with the features of MLZ helps to get the most out of the tool. (Most operations in MLZ work exactly as they do in official Zotero: for guidance on basic operation, the screencasts hosted on zotero.org are a good starting point.)

Adding items automagically

MLZ and Zotero are able to create database entries automatically from many publisher and aggregator websites, which can be identified by a small icon that appears to the right in the browser address bar. The icon shows that the site is recognised by one of the Zotero "site translators", small programs maintained by the Zotero community that extract metadata from particular web pages for storage in a Zotero database. MLZ is capable of capturing multilingual data directly from sites that supply it.[59]

To see multilingual captures in action, visit the CiNii service at http://ci.nii.ac.jp/. After running a search, a folder icon will show at

---

[57] See http://citationstylist.org

[58] BILLY BRAGG, *A13: Trunk Road to the Sea*, *on* THE PEEL SESSIONS (Strange Fruit 1991), *available at* http://www.youtube.com/watch?v=QO_CT3mcKrM.

[59] Concerning legal support, see page 15 above. For MLZ JavaScript functions useful in building site translators with multilingual support, see page 39 below.

the right end of the Firefox address bar. Click on the icon, select one or more items, and click $\boxed{\text{OK}}$ to add the items to your library. Alternatively, click on a search result, then click on the item icon (as shown on the previous page).

As detailed in the Appendices, the field assignments for legal item types in MLZ differ from mainstream Zotero. The MLZ site translators handle content accordingly, placing metadata in the fields appropriate to MLZ and the CSL-M styles. As of this writing, five law sites are covered by MLZ-specific translators: Google Scholar, BaiLII, CanLII, Cornell LII, and JuriCaf. Contribution of additional translators is welcome.[60]

Adding items manually

Items not found on the Web can be entered manually using the green ◉ icon in the MLZ interface. Clicking on the icon opens a menu listing the item types, with the most recently used types at the top. Select an item to open an MLZ item of the corresponding type (as shown in Figure 2.2 below). Clicking on any field will open it for editing. When manually entering data, and when editing database fields generally, clicking away from a field will save its content to the database automatically (there is no "Save" button—and no need for one).

Figure 2.2: The MLZ interface with an empty entry open in the right column.

Section as locator

For statutory item types,[61] a pinpoint locator can be set in the Section field. See page 34 below for details.

Special fields: Jurisdiction and Court

Several of the citation forms supported by the CSL-M styles (particularly for law) require fields that are not currently available in official CSL and mainstream

---

[60]Note that the terms of service attached to some legal information services may affect translator development or the distribution of translators.

[61]The "statutory" types are: Bill, Gazette, Statute, Regulation and Treaty.

Zotero. All fields supported by MLZ are documented in the *Field Examples* appendix. The behaviour of two is worth special mention.

The Jurisdiction field shows the jurisdiction of primary legal sources. Clicking on the field opens a search  box. Selecting an item from the search list after typing a portion of the jurisdiction name will set the value in the field.

The Court field is handled as an institution name. Institutional subunits are separated by a vertical bar (the field separator character |), beginning with the largest unit:

```
High Court|Queen's Bench
```

The content of the field can be transformed using the Abbreviation Filter. See page 34 below for details.

Sync preference panel

The citation data in a Zotero or MLZ database can be stored "in the cloud" via the Zotero Sync service. The service also supports sync of a small number of PDF and other attachment files (up to 300 megabytes), with extended storage available for a modest fee. Unless you have an exceptional need for data security, setting up sync of attachments as well as item metadata is a prudent thing to do, and a necessary step in setting up a collaborative research environment.[62]

Begin by visiting zotero.org and creating a free account, if you have not already done so. Click on the gear icon in the MLZ toolbar, select Preferences from the menu, and open the [Sync] preferences tab. Type your ID and password into the corresponding fields. Use the tick-box below the password field to choose whether to sync automatically, or only  when the green sync icon in the MLZ toolbar is clicked. Close the popup panel and you should be all set.

Locating the MLZ database

As lawyers say, it is good policy to trust and verify. Before putting MLZ to serious use, you will want to identify where your library data is stored on your computer. As the behaviour of MLZ is identical to Zotero, the guidance notes on the Zotero website at the following address are a good reference:

```
http://www.zotero.org/support/zotero_data
```

---

[62]The 300-megabyte limit applies to attachment files only. There is no limit on the volume of citation data that can be synced via the service.

After locating the `zotero` data folder on your computer, you should work out a method of making regular backup copies of its content (and its subfolders). It is hard to stress this point too strongly; backups are not something to trust to fate. In the way of things, the day will come when you turn the switch on your computer and nothing happens. To guard against that eventuality, be sure that you have a backup strategy in place (for your MLZ database certainly, but for other important files as well). Test your setup to be sure that when it is eventually needed, it will perform as expected.

Setting the item language

The Language field in an MLZ item indicates the language of the target resource. This is important metadata, and the field should ideally be set on all items; but it is particularly important to do so in multilingual environments.

Set the field to the two-character language code designated by the ISO 639-1 specification.[63] If the code of a right-to-left (RTL) language is set in this field, the fields in the item panel of the MLZ interface will switch to RTL mode.

Languages preference panel

A unique feature of MLZ is the ability to add multilingual variants—transliterations, translations and sort keys—for use in generating finished citations. When MLZ is run for the first time, the list of available variants (shown in Figure 2.3 on the following page) will be empty. Add a language by typing the (English) name of a base language into the search box, selecting it from the drop-down list. Add a transliteration method (e.g. `ja-Hira` or `ja-alalc97`) by clicking on the ⊕ plus button of a base language and selecting the transliteration method from the Script and Variant sub-menus.

In the preference panel, language codes for each variant are listed in the Tag column.[64] The Nickname col-

umn defaults to the code value: descriptive names can be entered by clicking on each entry.

---

[63] See http://en.wikipedia.org/wiki/List_of_ISO_639-1_codes

[64] MLZ language variant tags conform to A. Phillips & M. Davis, Tags for Identifying Languages, RFC 5646 (IETF, Network Working Group 2009).

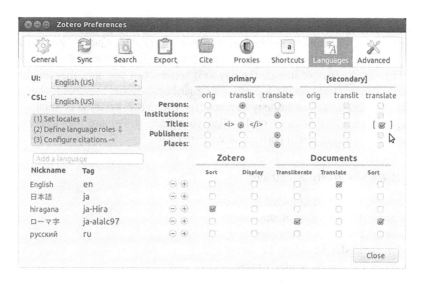

Figure 2.3: Language preferences with highlighted language role

Assign a field variant for use in citations in two steps. First, select a role for the variant by ticking its box in the Transliterate, Translate or Sort column of the languages list. Second, in the upper section of the panel, select the position in which each role should be applied within citations.

The [primary] selections simply substitute a language variant corresponding to the selected role for the original text, if a variant is available. The optional [secondary] selections are added immediately after the text of the target field. Primary Transliterate selections can be set to italics (using a pull-down menu that appears when the selection is left-clicked). Secondary selections can be enclosed in square or round brackets, or they can be set off from the primary entry with a comma.

Multilingual fields

Multilingual features are available on creators, and on ordinary text fields that reveal an outline around the field label when the cursor is hovered over it (as shown to the right). Right-clicking the label opens an Add Subfield menu. Use this to add fields for translations or transliterations of the headline field content. Left-clicking on an ordinary field opens a Reset Language menu (on creator labels, it is a submenu).

The multilingual menus list variants by their nicknames. When adding a field via the Add Subfield menu, select a variant from the list to open a new

field for it below the headline field, as shown in the insert. The steps are the same for Author and the other creator fields.[65]

To change the variant name on an existing field (including the headline field), use left-click to open the Reset Language menu. To remove an ordinary subfield, open it for editing and remove its content; the field will disappear. To remove a creator subfield, click on its ⊖ minus button.

Language control in word processor documents

When a new word processor document is opened with MLZ running in the background, it receives a copy of the current language preferences. Once created, a document's language settings can be controlled independently, from within the word processor plugin.[66] Document language settings can be found in the document preferences popup: click on the 🔲 menu button[67] and select the ⌞Languages⌟ tab from the top of the popup dialog. This will display a simplified version of the settings panel shown in Figure 2.3.

Using abbreviations

The Abbreviation Filter is an important companion to the CSL-M citation styles. In addition to abbreviating journal titles and court names, the Filter can be used to suppress redundant citation details (such as the court name in Shelton v. Tucker, 364 U.S. 479 [1960]), and to expand internal country codes into human-readable country names (e.g. converting jp to "Japan").

To test that the Abbreviation Filter is working, open a word processor document, select an MLZ style, and insert a citation to a Journal Article or a Case. If the journal or reporter is known to the plugin, it will be abbreviated automatically in the citation (hint: the abbreviation sets for each of the six CSL-M styles contain an entry for "Butterworths Medico-Legal Reports").

The operation of the Abbreviation Filter is explained in greater detail at page 34 below.

---

[65] As in official Zotero, entirely new creators are added with the ⊕ button, and the creator role can be changed to Editor, Translator et cetera with a left-click on the label.

[66] Language variants that you add via the MLZ Language Preferences Panel will be reflected in the document, but the other document language settings are independent of the MLZ Client.

[67] See page 21 above for the location of the Zotero menu in your word processor.

Getting Help

> *Up sprang that cowboy fireman*
> *And a gallant lad was he*
> *"Now I will save that baby*
> *If I wreck the whole SP"*
>
> —Harry McClintock[68]

MLZ is a work in progress. The system may have rough edges that you would like to see smoothed off, or lack facilities that you would like to see added. Some features may simply need to be explained more clearly. The first step to getting answers is choosing a channel for your query.

For general information about aspects of MLZ that are shared with Zotero, zotero.org is the first place to look for guidance. For everything related to the word processor plugins (including installation issues), for tips on organizing research materials, for questions about what Zotero (and by extension MLZ) is *for*, the Quick Links heading under the Documentation tab on the Zotero site is an excellent source of information.

For questions specific to MLZ, check the Errata tab on the CitationStylist project website to see whether your query has already been addressed:

        http://citationstylist.org/errata

This page will be updated periodically with answers to specific queries, responses to development requests, and errata to the text of this book. If you do not find an answer there, the next step is to post a query to the Zotero forums:

        http://forums.zotero.org/

When posting to the forums, flag your post with "[mlz]" at the start of the subject line, as shown in Figure 2.4.

Apart from making a speedy response more likely, flagging MLZ-specific issues in this way is an important courtesy to the community. The core Zotero developers are exclusively concerned with the stability and design of mainstream Zotero (as we all want them to be). MLZ issues should be fielded by the MLZ community, without consuming the attention of the core team.

If you find something that is broken or not working, you may be asked to determine whether the problem is specific to MLZ, or also affects mainstream Zotero. You can do this by installing mainstream Zotero in an alternate Firefox profile. Information on Firefox profiles is available at the following URL:

        https://support.mozilla.org/en-US/kb/profile-manager-
        create-and-remove-firefox-profiles

After starting Firefox in an alternative profile, install official Zotero in the usual way. The freshly-installed Zotero will issue a prompt asking whether you would

---

[68]Harry McClintock, The Trusty Lariat (Culver City, California, Victor 1930), *available at* http://www.youtube.com/watch?v=unmWIfSHN5c.

like to use your existing data directory. Click on [No] to create a separate, Zotero-compatible database for testing and comparison.

In addition to the formal channels above, feel free to contact me directly: my contact details are listed on the CitationStylist website.[69] I am always happy to hear about issues with the software; that is how things improve. The long-term aim for MLZ, as noted in the ReadMe link in the client itself, is to merge multilingual and legal functionality into official Zotero, with smooth migration of user data. As of this writing MLZ is not supported by a cast of thousands, but the system does work, and with a bit of communication, a bit of time, and a bit of funding here and there, communities do grow.

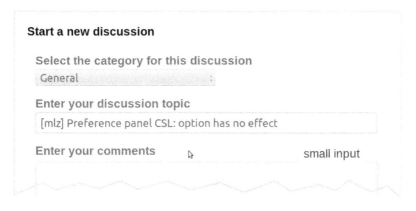

Figure 2.4: Starting a forum post on an MLZ-specific issue

---

[69] See http://citationstylist.org.

Chapter 3

Under the Bonnet

> *It's got a four-barrel carb and dual exhaust*
> *Four-eleven gears, you can really get lost*
> *It's got safety tubes and I'm not scared*
> *The brakes are good, the tires are fair*
>
> —Charlie Ryan[70]

MLZ and Zotero

As explained in the previous chapter, MLZ and Zotero are close relatives, but not perfect drop-in replacements for one another. Some of the differences between the two systems are described below.

CSL-M styles

The official CSL Style Repository[71] offers a large selection of styles written in the Citation Style Language (CSL). Like any language, CSL has grammatical rules, and these are described in two documents: a computer-friendly schema;[72] and a human-friendly specification.[73] The schema can be used to *validate* a style, confirming that it is grammatically correct. Official CSL styles are validated before they appear in the Repository.

To support legal writing, MLZ uses styles written in an extended version of the CSL language (CSL-M). These styles follow a slightly different grammar, defined in a separate schema and Specification Supplement,[74]. CSL-M styles are validated against their own schema before they are made available via the

---

[70]CHARLIE RYAN, HOT ROD LINCOLN (4-Star 1959), *available at* http://www.youtube.com /watch?v=8MS9fk1u6kA.

[71]The official CSL styles are available through the Zotero Style Repository located at http://zotero.org/styles.

[72]See https://github.com/citation-style-language/schema

[73]Rintze M. Zelle, Citation Style Language 1.0.1: Language Specification (Sep. 3, 2012), http://citationstyles.org/downloads/specification.html.

[74]Frank G. Bennett, CSL-M Specification Supplement (Sep. 29, 2011), http://gsl-nagoya-u.net /http/pub/citeproc-js-csl.html.

CitationStylist website.[75] The CSL-M family of styles will not work properly with official Zotero: if you are doing legal writing, you should use MLZ with a CSL-M style.

Database compatibility

Like Zotero, MLZ stores references as a set of *items*, collected in a personal or shared group library. Item content is stored in the MLZ data directory on your computer, in two places.[76] The descriptive *metadata* (title, author, date of publication, et cetera) is stored in a database file (zotero.sqlite). PDF files and other *item attachments* are stored in a subfolder (storage).

When MLZ is installed, it replaces an existing Zotero Client and "upgrades" its database. The upgrade process adds some extra containers ("tables") for multilingual data, as well as some fields ("table columns") for legal item types. Once a local database is upgraded to MLZ it can no longer be accessed directly by official Zotero.[77]

Sync compatibility

Zotero libraries can be synchronised to your user account on the Zotero website at http://zotero.org. If you keep multiple copies of your MLZ library—one at work and one at home, for example—regular synchronization via the website will populate changes made on one machine to the others.

In addition to your personal library, your may create or join one or more group libraries on the Zotero website under your account. In the MLZ Client (as in Zotero), these are shown below "My Library", as a separate set of named libraries, one for each group. Group libraries are useful for collaborative research projects, as they permit multiple researchers to work from the same set of reference items, linked to shared documents.

ISBN	410101003X
URL	
Library Catalog	Amazon.com
Extra	mlzsync1:0397{"type":"book","multifields":{"main": {"title":"ja"},"_keys":{"edition": {"ja-alalc97":"Modernised edition"},"publisher": {"en":"Shinchōsha"},"title":{"en":"The Little Master","ja-alalc97":"Bottchan"}}."_lsts":{"edition": ["ja-alalc97"],"publisher":["en"],"title":["en","ja-alalc97"]}},"multicreators":{"0":{"_key": {"ja-alalc97": {"lastName":"Natsume","firstName":"Sōseki"}}."_lst": [],"fieldMode":""}}}
Tags	Literature

Sync is particularly likely to be useful in multilingual environments, and MLZ is compatible with the sync service offered at zotero.org. However, given the extended fields and multilingual field variants contained in MLZ data, a small adjustment is needed: some data in some records is converted to JSON format and placed in the Extra field, as shown above. This data appears in the

[75]See http://citationstylist.org/tools

[76]See http://www.zotero.org/support/zotero_data for instructions on now to locate your database and other files—the guidance notes there apply equally to Zotero and MLZ.

[77]Data can be shared between MLZ and an official Zotero Client by syncing both to the same Zotero group.

Extra field only when viewing MLZ items online on zotero.org, or when synced to an official Zotero Client. Entries will appear normally in MLZ.

Locator labels and locator dates

In looseleaf services common in law libraries, pages are often dated individually to show when that portion of the text was last updated. To address this requirement, a date may be specified in the locator field when citing to such a work, in the following form:

```
p. 15|2006-07-00 A-2
```

The date must be a hyphen-delimited numeric date in year-month-day order as shown in the example, with 00 standing for an empty day or month. Everything after the date (or everything after the vertical bar if there is no date), is stored in the CSL-M locator-revision variable. This example also illustrates the "shorthand" form of label locators: the p. in p. 15 signals that what follows is a page number, to be rendered in the form appropriate to the target style.

Locator label abbreviations

To expand on the example above, locator labels can be set using the abbreviation short-forms shown in Table 3.1. Labels are recognised (producing localised or pluralised labels as appropriate to the style and context) in the word processor plugin locator field, in the Section field of legal item types, and in the header of child notes (see page 40 below).

Label	Abbreviation	Label	Abbreviation
Article	art.	Paragraph	para.
Book	bk.	Subparagraph	subpara.
Chapter	ch.	Part	pt.
Subchapter	subch.	Rule	r.
Column	col.	Section	sec.
Figure	fig.	Subsection	subsec.
Folio	fol.	Sub-verbo	sv.
Line	l.	Schedule	sch.
Note	n.	Title	tit.
Issue	no.	Verse	vrs.
Opus	op.	Volume	vol.
Page	p. or pp.		

Table 3.1: In-field locator label abbreviations

When a label abbreviation is used at the beginning of a field, it overrides any label set (via the drop-down menu) in the word processor plugin.

Section as locator

Pinpoint details do not ordinarily form part of the main item metadata under the [Info] tab: this information is normally added in the word processor plugin via the locator field provided for that purpose. However, for statutes and similar material[78] it often makes sense to break the original "document" into cite-worthy elements, and enter each as a separate item in the MLZ database. This facilitates note-taking, tagging, cross-linking of related provisions, and efficient search among other things. MLZ enables this by making two changes to Zotero: (a) treating the content of the Section field as a pinpoint locator on statutory types; and (b) generating a "collective" hidden ID for provisions from the same source, to produce correctly formatted back-references.

The two methods can be combined: the precision of a cite can be fine-tuned by appending supplementary details in the locator itself. For example, a statutory reference to title 33, section 3841 of the U.S. Code will render as follows with a locator value of (c)(2)(B):

33 USC § 3841(c)(2)(B).

The in-field locator label abbreviations can be used in the middle of a locator string, and will be transformed into the form appropriate to the target style.

Abbreviation Filter

The Abbreviation Filter for Zotero and MLZ is a Firefox plugin that provides a flexible mechanism for abbreviating or transforming citation elements, without altering entries in the database. The plugin works by matching field content against an abbreviation list associated with the current style. Lists can be imported and exported, and installed list entries can be edited in the word processor via a dialog box. Pre-packaged lists supporting particular styles are maintained on the CitationStylist website.

Managing abbreviations

When installed, the Abbreviation Filter adds an [abbrevs.] button to the "Classic View" word-processor citation edit/insert dialog. Clicking on the button will open the popup shown in Figure 3.1. The button in the upper left area of the popup (Journals and Reporters in the illustration) opens a pull-down list of abbreviation categories, each offering a list of field entries (on the left) and corresponding abbreviations (on the right).

Clicking on an entry in the right column opens it for editing. Pressing the Enter key or clicking elsewhere saves the entry. Abbreviations are stored in a database maintained by the plugin (located in the Zotero or MLZ data directory), and are associated with the current style. Abbreviation lists do not sync to the

---

[78]Bill, Gazette, Statute, Regulation and Treaty.

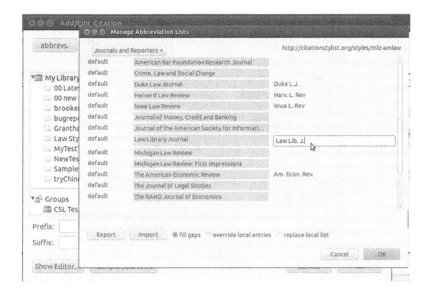

Figure 3.1: Abbreviations editor with a field open for editing

Zotero servers, but the lists for a style can be exported for sharing among users, machines or styles.

Abbreviation lists

Abbreviations are divided into several categories. Within each category, abbreviations are classified by Jurisdiction. Fields that originated from an item that has a Jurisdiction value (such as a Case) will show an entry for each level of specificity, ending in default. The list categories are:

Journals and Reporters This category covers journal abbreviations of all kinds.

Series Titles To avoid confusion between journal and series titles, series titles have their own separate category.

Titles This category covers ordinary titles, the names of legal judgments, and the many-purposed genre field.

Entire Institutions This and the Institution Parts category apply to names (such as Author) entered in single-field mode, and to the Publisher and Court fields. Institution parts should be entered from the largest to smallest unit, separated with "|" (vertical bar) characters.

This Entire Institutions abbreviation category is used to set the keys for content-neutral citations to law cases. For example, if the Court field contains `High Court|Chancery`, and the item is a neutral citation,[79] the key can be produced by setting the corresponding abbreviation to `UKHC`.

The abbreviated value returned by this transform may include one or more "|" (vertical bar) characters. The Institution Parts abbreviation (below) is applied after this transform.

Institution Parts Abbreviations registered in this category are applied to matching name parts of any institutional name, after the Entire Institution transform is applied.

Personal Nicknames Use this category to transform the author's own name, typically in citations to interviews and correspondence. For styles that require a placeholder such as "the author" in this case, enter that value here. The name can be suppressed in output altogether (in interview and correspondence items only) by entering a value of `{suppress}` (including the squiggly braces).

Places Use this for abbreviations of locations, such as "N.Y." for "New York". This category is also used to provide *expanded* forms of the CSL-M jurisdiction codes received by the processor (e.g. the code `is` can be set to render as `Iceland`).

Number field (strings) This category applies to *non*-numeric field content in a numeric variable.[80] For example, "Revised edition" in the Edition field would appear in this list, while a value of "2" would not.

Hereinafter Use this list to register short descriptive back-reference names for works with very long or ambiguous titles. Entries appear here only if `hereinafter` is supported by the style.

Classic Works This category is used for works that are commonly cited within a field, such as Blackstone's *Commentaries* (cited as "Bl Comm" in the OSCOLA style). Works appear in this category *only* if the item is of the Classic type, and the style supports this form of referencing. Items cited in this way will not be listed in the document bibliography.

Suppressing output

The Abbreviation Filter offers two methods of suppressing output. The use of `{suppress}` to suppress the author's own name in cites to interviews and correspondence is described above. It is also possible, in items of any type,

---

[79]That is, if the Reporter field is empty and the year of the decision is set in the Year As Vol. field. See page 56 below for an example.

[80]Relevant CSL-M variables include: `chapter-number`, `collection-number`, `edition`, `issue`, `locator`, `number`, `number-of-pages`, `number-of-volumes`, `page`, `volume`, and `citation-number`.

to suppress the output of *other* elements that follow the abbreviated element in rendering order.

For example, the *United States Reports* contain judgments of the United States Supreme Court exclusively. When citing for the benefit of an audience of lawyers, neither the Jurisdiction nor the Court (mapping to the `authority` variable in CSL-M) are needed in the cite. The following syntax will suppress both:

> `"U.S.": "!jurisdiction,authority>>>U.S."`

The exclamation point at the start of the field is programming shorthand for "exclude". The three angle braces separate the variable names from the actual abbreviation.

Importing abbreviation lists

Pre-packaged lists are available on the CitationStylist website.[81] Download a list by clicking on the ⎡Abbr⎤ button for the target style, saving the list to your desktop. Install the list through the word processor plugin by opening a citation in the target style, then opening the abbreviations popup with the ⎡**abbrevs.**⎤ button. Three options are available to control the effect of an import:

fill gaps This is the most "shy" method. Abbreviations will be added for the currently selected style only if they do not conflict with existing entries. Existing abbreviation settings will not be altered.

override local entries This will overwrite local entries where there is a conflict, but non-conflicting existing abbreviations will not be touched.

replace local list This is the most drastic method. All existing abbreviations for the currently selected style will be deleted before the imported list is installed.

Select an import method, and use the ⎡**Import**⎤ button to open the import dialog. Navigate to the file you saved in the previous step, and click Open to import the list.

Exporting abbreviation lists

Use the Export button in the abbreviations popup to export list data for the current style. Export currently ignores data in the `classic`, `nickname` and `hereinafter` segments.

---

[81] See `http://citationstylist.org/tools`

Hint lists

Lists provided under the [Hints] buttons on CitationStylist match *fragments* of a field, and are used to generate abbreviation suggestions for fields that have no registered entry. These lists can be imported, but their content is not editable through the plugin popup, and the import operation always completely overwrites the previous content of the list. If the abbreviation suggestions supplied by the plugin become a nuisance, phrase abbreviation can be turned off by installing an empty [Hints] list.[82]

Editing and Validating CSL-M Styles

CSL-M styles are provided via the CitationStylist website exclusively.[83] They cannot be released through the official CSL repository because they make use of small extensions to the CSL language that will not validate under the official CSL schema. The differences between the two language versions are documented in the CSL-M Specification Supplement,[84] and defined (for computers) in a companion schema. To check the syntax of a CSL-M style, use the dedicated validator at this address:

```
http://fbennett.github.io/csl-validator.js
```

Unfortunately, the user-friendly style editor for official CSL[85] will not work with CSL-M styles: but otherwise the general guidance offered in *Editing CSL Styles: Step-by-Step Guide* on the Zotero website[86] applies equally to CSL-M. In lieu of the style editor, a simple test pane embedded in Zotero and MLZ provides a means of previewing changes.[87] To use it, select one or more items in the center panel of MLZ, click on the ⚙ gear icon, choose Preferences, select the Advanced tab, and click on the Open CSL Editor button at the bottom.

Selecting a style displays sample output in the bottom section of the pane, rendered with the current language settings. General guidance on using the test pane is offered on the Zotero website. Be sure to save your work regularly by pasting it to a separate file when making changes in the test pane.

---

[82]For a downloadable empty list, see http://citationstylist/

[83]See http://citationstylist.org/

[84]*See* Zelle, Citation Style Language 1.0.1: Language Specification, *supra* note 73; *and* Bennett, CSL-M Specification Supplement, *supra* note 74.

[85]See http://editor.citationstyles.org/

[86]See http://www.zotero.org/support/dev/citation_styles /style_editing_step-by-step

[87]See http://www.zotero.org/support/dev/citation_styles /reference_test_pane

Site Translators

The magic download icon that appears in the Firefox address bar for many websites when Zotero or MLZ are installed is driven by a large set of "site translators", small snippets of JavaScript code that extract data from a browser page and store it in the Zotero or MLZ database. Detailed discussion of site translators is beyond the scope of this book, but extensive documentation is available through other channels. Documentation for developers is available on `zotero` `.org`.[88] Technical questions should be directed to the `zotero-dev` mailing list.[89]

MLZ provides two helper functions for use in constructing multilingual translators. Their usage is described below. Note that these are available only in MLZ: translators that use them will not work in mainstream Zotero.

setMultiField()

When storing multilingual fields extracted from a page, begin by setting the main value (the top-level default value) of the field using this function. The `lang` value is optional the first time a given field is set on an item; if `lang` has a value, it will be set explicitly as the default language of the field:

```
var ZU = Zotero.Utilities;
var fieldName = "title";
var val = "我輩は猫である";
var lang = "ja";
ZU.setMultiField(newItem, fieldName, val, lang);
```

Subsequent values saved to the same field of the item *must* carry a `lang` value:

```
val = "Wagahai wa neko de aru";
lang = "ja-alalc97";
ZU.setMultiField(newItem, fieldName, val, lang);
```

When the item is saved, values after the first will show up in the MLZ interface as field variants, each labeled with its respective language tag (or with its nickname, if one has been set by the user).

setMultiCreator()

Multilingual creators are handled in a similar fashion. Again the default language is stored first, as shown in the code samples on the following page (using `cleanAuthor` to generate creator objects).

---

[88]One particularly useful resource for MLZ translator authors is the field mapping table at `http://fbennett.github.io/z2csl/diffMap.html`.

[89]To subscribe, visit `http://groups.google.com/group/zotero-dev`.

```
var ZU = Zotero.Utilities;
var type = "author";
var str = "夏目，漱石";
var lang = "ja";
var newName = ZU.cleanAuthor(str, type, true);
ZU.setMultiCreator(newName, newName, lang, type);
```

Here again, the `lang` value is optional the first time a creator is stored on the object. Subsequent variants stored on the object *must* have a `lang` value:

```
str = "Natsume, Sōseki";
lang = "ja-alalc97";
var altName = ZU.cleanAuthor(str, type, true);
ZU.setMultiCreator(newName, altName, lang, type);
```

Note that the initial creator is passed as the first argument to the function when setting variants of the name. The composite creator (`newName` in this example) can be attached to the translator item in the usual way.

Scannable Cite Markers

Zotero and MLZ are powerful tools for managing durable personal library collections. Site translators provide a convenient way to collect material. The word-processor plugins tie libraries directly into the final writing process. For the middle stage of research, Zotero and MLZ offer tagging and note-taking, but separate outlining, mind-mapping and brainstorming programs offer powerful alternatives.

To use such tools efficiently, you will want to embed MLZ-aware, Zotero-aware citations in your notes at an early stage. Full Zotero integration is limited to Word and LibreOffice Writer, but with *scannable cite markers*, MLZ or Zotero can be used with many other programs. The only requirement is that the document containing scannable cite markers be ultimately converted to Open Document Format (ODF), the native file format of LibreOffice Writer.

To get started using scannable cite markers, visit the project website in Firefox and install the RTF/ODF Scanner plugin:

```
http://zotero-odf-scan.github.io/zotero-odf-scan/
```

After installing the plugin, you can add MLZ references to your notes and documents by following these steps:

- From the gear menu, open the Export tab in Preferences, and set the Scannable Cites export translator as the Default Output Format.

- Copy citations into a document by pressing the shift key and dragging items, or by copying items to the clipboard with Ctrl + Alt + C (Shift + Cmd + C on Mac) and then pasting them into the document.

- Save your document in ODF format.

- From the ⚙ gear menu, open the **RTF/ODF Scan** wizard, choose "ODF (citations)" conversion, select your document as the input file, set an output file, and press ⃞ Next ⃞ to perform the conversion.

- Open the document and select an in-text style such as "Chicago (author-date)". Click the ⟳ refresh button in the word processor to complete the conversion. You may now select another style, and carry on editing in LibreOffice Writer.

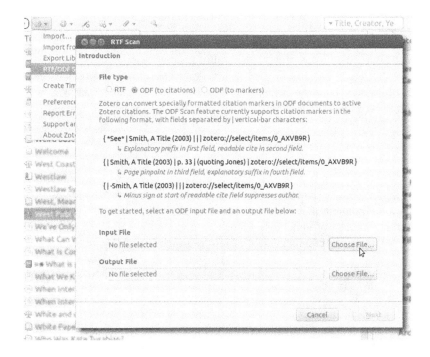

Figure 3.2: Running the RTF/ODF Scan conversion utility

Scannable cite format

Scannable Zotero/MLZ citation markers identify items in the Zotero database using a unique key that looks something like this:

```
zg:148698:DGTREJVQ
```

In this example, the z indicates that the item is from Zotero (or MLZ). The g indicates that it is a group library (user libraries are marked with u). The number identifies the specific library containing the item, and the final string of characters identifies the item within the library. Do not edit the key: it is used by the plugin to convert the scannable cite to a "live" Zotero/MLZ citation.

The Scannable Cites export translator includes basic information about the item, as shown below. Scannable cites are composed of five fields, divided by "|" (vertical bar) characters, and enclosed overall in squiggly braces:

```
{ |Hardin, Tragedy of the Commons, 1968
 | | |zg:148698:DGTREJVQ}
```

Affixes can be added in the first and fourth fields, and a pinpoint can be added in the third.

The Scannable Cites export trans-   ☑ Include Zotero link wrappers in QuickCopy citations
lator and the RTF/ODF Scanner work
both with MLZ and official Zotero.
As an alternative, MLZ offers a method of generating references directly from notes attached to an item. To enable it, visit the ⸢Export⸥ tab of Preferences, select a bibliographic style as the Default Output Format, then find the tick-box shown in the inset above, and select it. After "link wrappers" are enabled, copying an item from the centre panel will insert a reference in the same scannable format, using the selected style for the item description:

```
{ | Hardin 1968 | | |zg:148698:DGTREJVQ}
```

A pinpoint[90] and a quotation or comment can be included at the top of a child note. The pinpoint must be the first line of the note, followed by the lines of either a comment or quotation. Lines of a quotation are prefixed by an equals sign (=), lines of a comment are prefixed by a tilde (~):

```
p. 1243
= We want the maximum good per person;
= but what is good?
```

When the note above is shift-dragged into a text editor, the pinpoint and quotation will be included:

```
{ |Hardin 1968 | p. 1243 | ("We want the maximum
good per person; but what is good?") |
zg:148698:DGTREJVQ}
```

Prefixing comment lines with a tilde (~) instead of a = equals sign will yield a comment without quote marks:

```
{ |Hardin 1968 | p. 1243 | (arguing that problems
of market failure are commonly overlooked) |
zg:148698:DGTREJVQ}
```

---

[90]Pinpoints are set by using a leading label abbreviation. Recognised abbreviations are listed above at page 33.

Appendix A

Item Examples

The examples below illustrate data input and citation forms for particular resources. In each example, a double box encloses the item type name from the MLZ interface (e.g. **Artwork**) and CSL-M (e.g. `graphic`). MLZ field labels are set in boldface, with the CSL-M variable name to the right.

Artwork: Paintings, Photos, Sculptures

Artwork `graphic`	**Artwork Size** `dimensions` *Drawing in*
	500 px × 271 px *Collection*

Title `title`
Wikipedian Protester

Website Title `container-title`
XKCD

Artist `author`
| Munroe | Randall |

Date `issued`
2007-08

Medium `medium`
Online cartoon

URL `URL`
http://xkcd.com/285/

American Law `first` reference
> Randall Munroe, *Wikipedian Protester*, XKCD (Online cartoon, 500 px × 271 px, Aug. 2007), http://xkcd.com/285/.

The citations above refer to the cartoon to the right. (The license terms permit its use in "books, blogs, newsletters, and presentations", so here it is.) For one-off online artworks or photos that are not part of a collection use **Webpage** instead (page 92 below).

Museum Piece	**Artwork** `graphic`	**Artwork Size** `dimensions`
		77 cm × 53 cm

Title `title`
Mona Lisa

Date `issued`
1503-1519

Artist `author`
Leonardo da Vinci

Archive `archive`
Musée du Louvre

Medium `medium`
Oil on poplar

American Law `first` reference
> Leonardo da Vinci, *Mona Lisa* (Oil on poplar, 77 cm × 53 cm, *in* Musée du Louvre, 1503–1519).

The Artwork type can be used for any artifact, including sculptures, installations, photographs, graffiti ...

Articles

Per-Issue Pagination	**Magazine Article** `article-magazine`	**Volume** `volume`
		49

Title `title`
The Optimal Number of Friends in the Information Age

Issue `issue`
4

Date `issued`
2005-07

Author `author`
Ozaktas   Haldun

Pages `page`
32

Publication `container-title`
Journal of Irreproducible Results

OSCOLA `first` reference
> Haldun Ozaktas, 'The Optimal Number of Friends in the Information Age' (2005) 49(4) J Irreproducible Results 32

American Law `first` reference
> Haldun Ozaktas, *The Optimal Number of Friends in the Information Age*, 49 J. IRREPRODUCIBLE RESULTS, Jul. 2005, at 32.

Articles in journals with separate pagination for each issue can be set to the Magazine Article type.

Journal Article
`article-journal`

Title `title`

Organised crime: A social
network approach

Author `author`

| McIllwain | Jeffrey Scott |

Publication `container-title`

Crime, Law and Social Change

Volume `volume` *Continuous*

32

Pagination
within each

Issue `issue` *Volume*

4

Pages `page`

301-323

Date `issued`

1999

American Law `first` reference

Jeffrey Scott McIllwain, *Organised Crime: A Social Network
Approach*, 32 CRIME, L. & SOC. CHANGE 301 (1999).

American Law `subsequent` reference

McIllwain, *supra* note 1.

New Zealand Law `first` reference

Jeffrey Scott McIllwain "Organised crime: A social network
approach" (1999) 32 Crime, L & Soc Change 301.

New Zealand Law `subsequent` reference

McIllwain, above n 1.

McGill Guide (English) `first` reference

Jeffrey Scott McIllwain, "Organised Crime: A Social Network
Approach" (1999) 32:4 Crime, Law and Social Change 301.

McGill Guide (English) `subsequent` reference

McIllwain, "Organised Crime: A Social Network Approach", *supra*
note 1.

Chicago Full Note `first` reference

Jeffrey Scott McIllwain, "Organised Crime: A Social Network
Approach," *Crime, Law and Social Change* 32, no. 4 (1999): 301–23.

Chicago Full Note `subsequent` reference

McIllwain, "Organised Crime: A Social Network Approach."

The Journal Article type is appropriate when the pagination of the journal is
continuous across the numbers comprising a volume. In the example above, note
use of the full page range in the Pages field; this should generally be included
in the item data, since some styles (such as Chicago) do require it.

For items with non-continuous pagination, use the Magazine Article type,
shown on the facing page.

Audio Recordings and Musical Scores

Album | **Audio Recording** | **Format**   medium
Track | song | [Vinyl LP]

Title   title   **Label/Publisher**   publisher
[Little Umbrellas]   [Bizarre Records]

Performer   author   **Date**   issued
[Zappa] [Frank]   [1969]

Album   container-title
[Hot Rats]

> American Law first reference
> FRANK ZAPPA, *Little Umbrellas, on* HOT RATS (Vinyl LP, Bizarre
> Records 1969).
> American Law ibid reference
> *Id.*

A pattern for popular music. Singles will of course have no Album value.

Classical | **Audio Recording** | **Album**   container-title
Track with | song | [1812 Overture etc.]
Composer |

Title   title   **Format**   medium
[1812 Overture]   [CD]

Performer   author   **Label/Publisher**   publisher
[Ozawa] [Seiji]   [EMI Angel]

Performer   author   **Date**   issued
[Berlin Philharmonic]   [1990]

Composer   composer
[Tchaikovsky] [Pyotr Il'yich]

> New Zealand Law first reference
> Seiji Ozawa, Berlin Philharmonic "1812 Overture" on *1812 Overture
> etc* (CD, EMI Angel, 1990).
>
> American Law first reference
> SEIJI OZAWA, BERLIN PHILHARMONIC, *1812 Overture*
> [Tchaikovsky], *on* 1812 OVERTURE ETC. (CD, EMI Angel 1990).

These cite forms suit my layman's eye, but I am known to be tone deaf, and
reasonable minds may differ. Omit any fields not relevant to the target resource.

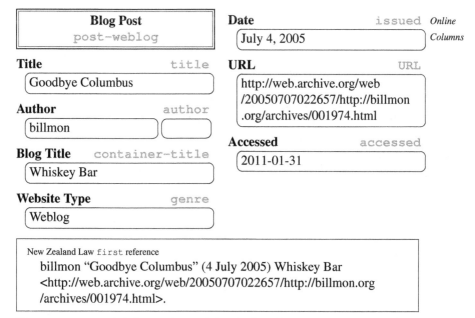

Audio Recording		Label/Publisher	`publisher`	*Musical Score*
`song`		P. Jurgenson		

Title `title`
The Year 1812

Date `issued`
1882

Composer `composer`
Tchaikovsky · Pyotr Il'yich

Opus No. `section`
op. 49

Place `publisher-place`
Moscow

Orig. Date `original-date`
1880

American Law `first` reference
PYOTR IL'YICH TCHAIKOVSKY, THE YEAR 1812, Op. 49 (Moscow, P. Jurgenson 1882).

American Law `subsequent` reference
TCHAIKOVSKY, *supra* note 1.

Sheet music will have a Composer, and possibly a Label/Publisher and Place, but no Performer.

Blog Posts

Blog Post	Date	`issued`	*Online Columns*
`post-weblog`	July 4, 2005		

Title `title`
Goodbye Columbus

URL `URL`
http://web.archive.org/web/20050707022657/http://billmon.org/archives/001974.html

Author `author`
billmon

Accessed `accessed`
2011-01-31

Blog Title `container-title`
Whiskey Bar

Website Type `genre`
Weblog

New Zealand Law `first` reference
billmon "Goodbye Columbus" (4 July 2005) Whiskey Bar <http://web.archive.org/web/20050707022657/http://billmon.org/archives/001974.html>.

Blog posts are straightforward materials, cited as shown above. A URL should, of course, normally be provided.

Books

Simple Book Cite

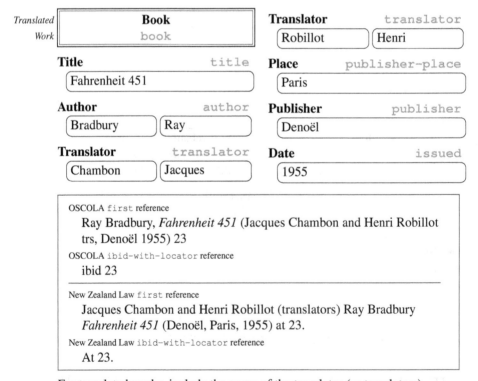

| **Book** |
| book |

Title `title`
Fahrenheit 451

Author `author`
Bradbury | Ray

Place `publisher-place`
New York

Publisher `publisher`
Ballantine Books

Date `issued`
1953

American Law `first` reference
RAY BRADBURY, FAHRENHEIT 451 (Ballantine Books 1953).

Chicago Full Note `first` reference
Ray Bradbury, *Fahrenheit 451* (New York: Ballantine Books, 1953).

The Place of publication has been suppressed in the American Law example using the Abbreviation Filter (see page 34 above).

Translated Work

| **Book** |
| book |

Title `title`
Fahrenheit 451

Author `author`
Bradbury | Ray

Translator `translator`
Chambon | Jacques

Translator `translator`
Robillot | Henri

Place `publisher-place`
Paris

Publisher `publisher`
Denoël

Date `issued`
1955

OSCOLA `first` reference
Ray Bradbury, *Fahrenheit 451* (Jacques Chambon and Henri Robillot trs, Denoël 1955) 23

OSCOLA `ibid-with-locator` reference
ibid 23

New Zealand Law `first` reference
Jacques Chambon and Henri Robillot (translators) Ray Bradbury *Fahrenheit 451* (Denoël, Paris, 1955) at 23.

New Zealand Law `ibid-with-locator` reference
At 23.

For translated works, include the name of the translator (or translators).

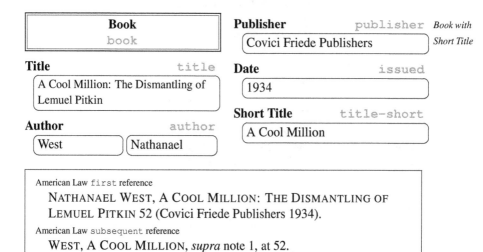

| Book | | Place | publisher-place | *Book with* |
| book | | Sausalito, California | | *Editor* |

Title *title*
Tough trip through Paradise
1878-1879

Publisher *publisher*
Comstock Editions

Date *issued*
1986

Author *author*
Garcia | Andrew

ISBN *ISBN*
9780891740087

Editor *editor*
Stein | Bennett H.

McGill Guide (French) first reference
   Andrew Garcia, *Tough trip through Paradise 1878-1879*, Bennett H
   Stein, dir, Sausalito, California, Comstock Editions, 1986, à la p 99.
McGill Guide (French) ibid-with-locator reference
   Ibid, à la p 99.

McGill Guide (English) first reference
   Andrew Garcia, *Tough Trip through Paradise 1878-1879* (Bennett H
   Stein, ed, Sausalito, California: Comstock Editions, 1986) at 99.
McGill Guide (English) ibid-with-locator reference
   Ibid, at 99.

Include the editor of an edited volume.

| Book | | Publisher | publisher | *Book with* |
| book | | Covici Friede Publishers | | *Short Title* |

Title *title*
A Cool Million: The Dismantling of
Lemuel Pitkin

Date *issued*
1934

Short Title *title-short*
A Cool Million

Author *author*
West | Nathanael

American Law first reference
   NATHANAEL WEST, A COOL MILLION: THE DISMANTLING OF
   LEMUEL PITKIN 52 (Covici Friede Publishers 1934).
American Law subsequent reference
   WEST, A COOL MILLION, *supra* note 1, at 52.

If used, the Short Title should match the main title portion of the Title field.
To set an abbreviated form of the title, use the Abbreviation Filter instead (see
page 34 above).

Book Chapters

Chapter in an Edited Volume

Book Section
chapter

Title   title

Continuing Seizure: Fourth Amendment Seizure in Section 1983 Malicious Prosecution Cases

Author   author

| Ferguson | Andrew G. |

Book Author   container-author

National Lawyers Guild

Editor   editor

| Saltzman | Steven |

Book Title   container-title

Civil Rights Litigation and Attorney Fees Annual Handbook

Volume   volume

15

Place   publisher-place

Chicago

Publisher   publisher

West

Date   issued

1999

Pages   page

54\-1

American Law first reference

Andrew G. Ferguson, *Continuing Seizure: Fourth Amendment Seizure in Section 1983 Malicious Prosecution Cases*, *in* 15 NAT'L LAWYERS GUILD, CIVIL RIGHTS LITIGATION AND ATTORNEY FEES ANNUAL HANDBOOK 54-1 (Steven Saltzman ed., 1999).

The Publisher has been suppressed via the Abbreviation Filter in this example (see page 34 above). A backslash prevents a hyphen from becoming an en-dash.

Chapter in a Sole-Authored Volume

Book Section
chapter

Title   title

Law in Science and Science in Law

Book Author   container-author

| Holmes | Oliver Wendell |

Book Title   container-title

Collected Legal Papers

Date   issued

1920

Pages   page

210

American Law first reference

OLIVER WENDELL HOLMES, *Law in Science and Science in Law*, *in* COLLECTED LEGAL PAPERS 210, 210 (1920).

Note the use of Book Author to distinguish chapters in books by a single author.

Cases: Federal Level or Unitary State

Case	Reporter	container-title *Nominate*
legal_case	Butterworths Medico-Legal Reports	*Report, Unique*

Case Name `title`
Barrett v. Enfield L.B.C.

Reporter Volume `volume` *Volume*
49 *Number*

Short Title `title-short`
Barrett

First Page `page`
1

Jurisdiction `jurisdiction`
United Kingdom

Date Decided `issued`
1999-06-17

Court `authority`
House of Lords

Date Published `publication-date`
1999

OSCOLA `first` reference
Barrett v Enfield LBC (1999) 49 BMLR 1 (HL)

OSCOLA `ibid-with-locator` reference
ibid 100

OSCOLA `subsequent` reference
Barrett (n 1)

American Law `first` reference
Barrett v. Enfield L.B.C., (1999) 49 B.M.L.R. 1 (HL).

American Law `ibid-with-locator` reference
Id. at 100.

American Law `subsequent` reference
Barrett, (1999) 49 B.M.L.R. 1.

Note the following special features of case items:

- A Jurisdiction value must *always* be provided: because case citation forms vary between jurisdictions, and the variations are relatively static across styles, an item without a Jurisdiction value may not format consistently. MLZ always supplies a value in this field.

- In MLZ, the Date Decided (mapping to `issued`) is supplemented for published cases by a Date Published value (mapping to `publication-date` in CSL-M).

- The Court field (mapping to `authority` in CSL-M) is parsed and handled as an institutional name in all CSL-M styles.

This general form of entry applies to nominate reports of all national jurisdictions.

Nominate
Report,
Year as
Volume

Case	
legal_case	

Case Name   title

Hopp v. Lepp

Jurisdiction   jurisdiction

Canada

Court   authority

Supreme Court

Reporter   container-title

Supreme Court Reports

Year As Vol.   collection-number

1980

Reporter Volume   volume

2

First Page   page

192

Date Decided   issued

1980-05-20

OSCOLA first reference
> *Hopp v Lepp* [1980] 2 SCR 192 [7]

OSCOLA subsequent reference
> *Hopp v Lepp* (n 1) [7]

American Law first reference
> Hopp v. Lepp, [1980] 2 S.C.R. 192, para. 7 (Can.).

American Law subsequent reference
> *Hopp v. Lepp*, [1980] 2 S.C.R. 192, para. 7.

Paragraph pinpoint and backreference forms may vary across styles.

Nominate
Report,
Year as
Volume,
Late
Publication

Case	
legal_case	

Case Name   title

Swiss Bank Corp. v. Air Canada

Jurisdiction   jurisdiction

Canada

Court   authority

Court of Appeal

Reporter   container-title

Federal Court Reports

Year As Vol.   collection-number

1988

Reporter Volume   volume

1

First Page   page

71

Date Decided   issued

1987

McGill Guide (English) first reference
> *Swiss Bank Corp v Air Canada* (1987), [1988] 1 FC 71 (Can CA).

In a Canadian nominate report citation, when the decision and publication dates differ, both are shown.

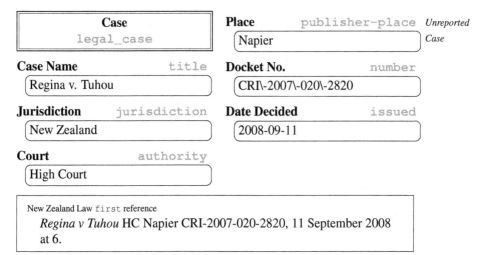

Case	
`legal_case`	
Case Name `title`	
MiningWatch Canada v. Canada (Fisheries and Oceans)	
Jurisdiction `jurisdiction`	
Canada	
Court `authority`	
Supreme Court	

Docket No. `number` *Vendor-Neutral Cite*
32797

Year As Vol. `collection-number`
2010

First Page `page`
2

Date Decided `issued`
2010-01-21

McGill Guide (French) `first` reference
MiningWatch Canada v Canada (Fisheries and Oceans), 2010 SCC 2 (Can).

"Neutral" citations identify the case itself, independent of any fixed nominate reporter. Such cites have the following special characteristics:

- No value is set in the Reporter field.

- Similar to nominate reports that set the year of publication as the volume number, the year of publication is set in the Year As Vol. field.

- The Abbreviation Filter is used to convert the value in the Court field to a court reference code ("SCC" in the example above).

Case	
`legal_case`	
Case Name `title`	
Regina v. Tuhou	
Jurisdiction `jurisdiction`	
New Zealand	
Court `authority`	
High Court	

Place `publisher-place` *Unreported Case*
Napier

Docket No. `number`
CRI\-2007\-020\-2820

Date Decided `issued`
2008-09-11

New Zealand Law `first` reference
Regina v Tuhou HC Napier CRI-2007-020-2820, 11 September 2008 at 6.

Unreported cases generally include a Docket Number and have no value for Year As Vol. or Reporter. Other fields such as Place (shown in this example), Filing Date, Reign, and Call No. may be relevant, depending on the jurisdiction. See pages 56 and 57 below for other examples.

Cases: Province, State or Subjurisdiction

Regional
Nominate
Reporter,
Unique
Volume
Number

Case
legal_case

Case Name   title

Chuck Wagon Catering Inc. v.
Raduege

Short Title   title-short

Chuck Wagon Catering

Jurisdiction   jurisdiction

Wisconsin, US

Court   authority

Supreme Court

Reporter   container-title

Northwest Reporter Second

Reporter Volume   volume

277

First Page   page

797

Date Decided   issued

1979-05-01

Date Published publication-date

1979

American Law first reference

Chuck Wagon Catering Inc. v. Raduege, 277 N.W.2d 797 (Wis. Sup. Ct. 1979).

The name of the state is included in American Law citations, if it is not obvious from the name of the reporter.

State-
Specific
Nominate
Reporter,
Unique
Volume
Number

Case
legal_case

Case Name   title

Chuck Wagon Catering Inc. v.
Raduege

Short Title   title-short

Chuck Wagon Catering

Jurisdiction   jurisdiction

Wisconsin, US

Court   authority

Supreme Court

Reporter   container-title

Wisconsin Reporter Second

Reporter Volume   volume

88

First Page   page

740

Date Decided   issued

1979-05-01

Date Published publication-date

1979

American Law first reference

Chuck Wagon Catering Inc. v. Raduege, 88 Wisc.2d 740 (1979).

Suppression of unwanted state names is handled by the Abbreviation Filter (see page 34 above).

Case
legal_case

Case Name   title
| Fucella v. Ricker |

Jurisdiction   jurisdiction
| Ontario, Canada |

Court   authority
| High Court of Justice |

Reporter   container-title   *Provincial*
| Ontario Reports Second | *Reporter,*

Unique

Reporter Volume   volume   *Volume*
| 35 | *Number*

First Page   page
| 423 |

Date Decided   issued
| 1982 |

OSCOLA first reference
Fucella v Ricker (1982) 35 OR (2d) 423 [7] (H Ct J)

American Law first reference
Fucella v. Ricker (1982), 35 O.R. (2d) 423, para. 7 (Ont. High Ct. J.).

When decisions by provincial courts are cited in a foreign style (and therefore to a foreign audience), a hint of the province or state name may be desired even where it would be deemed obvious to a domestic audience.

Case
legal_case

Case Name   title
| Bunt v. Tilley |

Jurisdiction   jurisdiction
| England and Wales, UK |

Court   authority
| High Court|Queen's Bench |

Reporter   container-title
| All England Reports |

Year As Vol.   collection-number   *General*
| 2006 | *Nominate*

Report,

Reporter Volume   volume   *Year as*
| 3 | *Volume*

Number

First Page   page
| 336 |

Date Decided   issued
| 2006-03-10 |

Date Published   publication-date
| 2006 |

OSCOLA first reference
Bunt v Tilley [2006] 3 All ER 336 (QB) [1–37]

American Law first reference
Bunt v. Tilley, [2006] 3 All E.R. 336 (QB) [1–37].

This example illustrates the use of the Volume field in items cited with the year as volume number, but published as multiple physical volumes within a given year.

Neutral
Citation

Case
`legal_case`

Case Name   `title`
Re Bernard L. Madoff Investment
Securities L.L.C.

Short Title   `title-short`
Bernard Madoff Securities

Jurisdiction   `jurisdiction`
England and Wales, UK

Court   `authority`
High Court|Chancery

Year As Vol.   `collection-number`
2009

First Page   `page`
442

Date Decided   `issued`
2009-02-27

> OSCOLA `first` reference
> *Re Bernard L Madoff Investment Securities LLC* [2009] EWHC 442
> (Ch)
> OSCOLA `subsequent+` reference
> *Bernard Madoff Securities* (n 1)

Neutral citations to regional courts differ from citations to a top-level court only in the value of the **Jurisdiction** field.

Slip
Opinion

Case
`legal_case`

Case Name   `title`
Kitchens v. Grohman

Jurisdiction   `jurisdiction`
D. Massachussetts, US (federal)

Court   `authority`
District Court

Docket No.   `number`
90\-345

Date Decided   `issued`
1990-12-04

> OSCOLA `first` reference
> *Kitchens v Grohman* No 90-345, slip op at 6 (D Mass 4 December
> 1990)
> OSCOLA `subsequent` reference
> *Kitchens v Grohman* (n 1) 6
>
> ---
>
> American Law `first` reference
> Kitchens v. Grohman, No. 90-345, slip op. at 6 (D. Mass. Dec. 4,
> 1990).
> American Law `subsequent` reference
> *Kitchens v. Grohman*, at 6.

"Slip opinions" (in U.S. legal vernacular) are equivalent to "unreported opinions" in other jurisdictions, and the fields used are the same.

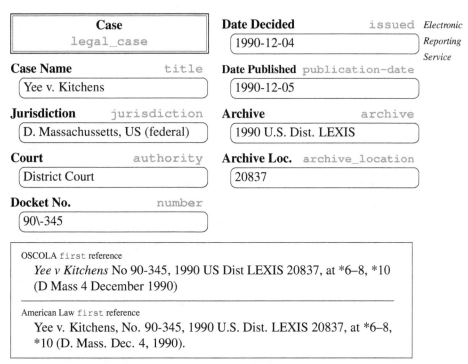

| **Case** | | **Place** publisher-place | *Unreported* |
| legal_case | | Nanaimo | *Case* |

| **Case Name** title | **Docket No.** number |
| Stephenson v. Stephenson | 5920/004143 |

| **Jurisdiction** jurisdiction | **Date Decided** issued |
| British Columbia, Canada | 1984-12-06 |

| **Court** authority |
| Supreme Court |

> OSCOLA first reference
> *Stephenson v Stephenson* (6 December 1984) Nanaimo 5920/004143
> [7] (BC SC)

Unreported citations to provincial, regional, state-level or subordinate federal courts differ from their top-level counterparts only in the Jurisdiction value. See page 53 above for another example.

Case		**Date Decided** issued	*Electronic*
legal_case		1990-12-04	*Reporting*
			Service

| **Case Name** title | **Date Published** publication-date |
| Yee v. Kitchens | 1990-12-05 |

| **Jurisdiction** jurisdiction | **Archive** archive |
| D. Massachussetts, US (federal) | 1990 U.S. Dist. LEXIS |

| **Court** authority | **Archive Loc.** archive_location |
| District Court | 20837 |

| **Docket No.** number |
| 90\-345 |

> OSCOLA first reference
> *Yee v Kitchens* No 90-345, 1990 US Dist LEXIS 20837, at *6–8, *10
> (D Mass 4 December 1990)
>
> ---
>
> American Law first reference
> Yee v. Kitchens, No. 90-345, 1990 U.S. Dist. LEXIS 20837, at *6–8,
> *10 (D. Mass. Dec. 4, 1990).

References to otherwise unpublished cases available via an electronic legal information service generally consist of a phrase specifying the service and database, and an identifier. CSL-M styles expect this information in the Archive and Archive Loc. fields.

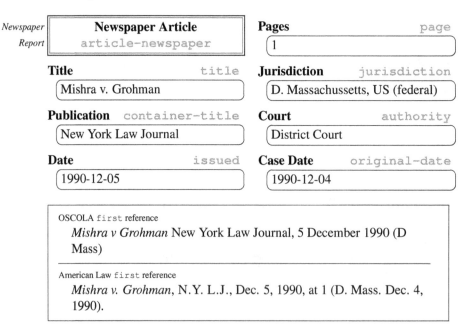

Looseleaf Services

Case
`legal_case`

Case Name   `title`
In re Looney

Jurisdiction   `jurisdiction`
W.D. Virginia, US (federal)

Court   `authority`
Bankruptcy Court

Reporter   `container-title`
Bankruptcy Law Reports (CCH)

Year As Vol.   `collection-number`
1987-1989

First page   `page`
para. 72,447

Date Decided   `issued`
1988-09-09

Supp. Name   `genre`
Transfer Binder

OSCOLA `first` reference

In re Looney [1987–89 Transfer Binder] Bankruptcy Law Reports (CCH) para 72,447, para 7 (Bankr WD Va 9 September 1988)

A case reference to a looseleaf service is not fundamentally different from one to a reporter. In the example above, note the use of the Supp. Name field, and the `para.` label abbreviation in the First Page field, which is interpreted by the citation processor.

Newspaper Report

Newspaper Article
`article-newspaper`

Title   `title`
Mishra v. Grohman

Publication   `container-title`
New York Law Journal

Date   `issued`
1990-12-05

Pages   `page`
1

Jurisdiction   `jurisdiction`
D. Massachussetts, US (federal)

Court   `authority`
District Court

Case Date   `original-date`
1990-12-04

OSCOLA `first` reference

Mishra v Grohman New York Law Journal, 5 December 1990 (D Mass)

American Law `first` reference

Mishra v. Grohman, N.Y. L.J., Dec. 5, 1990, at 1 (D. Mass. Dec. 4, 1990).

The Newspaper Article type can be used for case references by adding a supplementary Jurisdiction, plus the name of the court and date of the decision.

Classic Works

Classic		
classic		

Title	title
Commentaries	

Author	author
Blackstone	William

Volume	volume	*Standard*
2		*Commentary*

Date	issued
1765-1769	

OSCOLA first reference
2 Bl Comm

American Law first reference
2 WILLIAM BLACKSTONE, COMMENTARIES.

MLZ Classic items can be entirely rewritten via the Abbreviation Filter (page 34 above), and are omitted when generating a bibliography.

Computer Programs

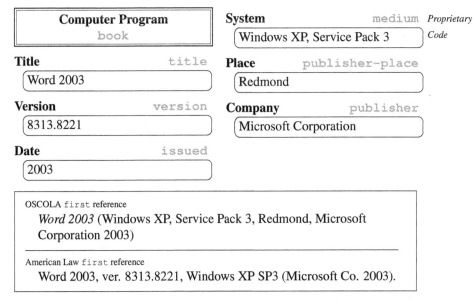

Computer Program		
book		

Title	title
Word 2003	

Version	version
8313.8221	

Date	issued
2003	

System	medium	*Proprietary*
Windows XP, Service Pack 3		*Code*

Place	publisher-place
Redmond	

Company	publisher
Microsoft Corporation	

OSCOLA first reference
Word 2003 (Windows XP, Service Pack 3, Redmond, Microsoft Corporation 2003)

American Law first reference
Word 2003, ver. 8313.8221, Windows XP SP3 (Microsoft Co. 2003).

The Computer Program citation forms here are things that I have concocted as a starting point. Suggestions for improvement are most certainly welcome.

Open Source Program

Computer Program	
book	

Title `title`
TₑX

Programmer `author`
Knuth | Donald

Version `version`
3.1415926

Date `issued`
February 2008

System `medium`
WEB

URL `URL`
http://www.tex.ac.uk/ctan/systems/knuth/dist/tex/tex.web

Accessed `accessed`
2012-02-04

OSCOLA `first` reference
    Donald Knuth, *TₑX* (WEB, 2008)

American Law `first` reference
    Donald Knuth, TₑX, ver. 3.1415926, WEB (Feb. 2008), http://www.tex.ac.uk/ctan/systems/knuth/dist/tex/tex.web.

Chicago Full Note `first` reference
    Donald Knuth, *TₑX*, WEB, 2008, http://www.tex.ac.uk/ctan/systems/knuth/dist/tex/tex.web (accessed February 4, 2012).

Named Versions

Computer Program	
book	

Title `title`
Ubuntu

Version `version`
Natty Narwal

Date `issued`
April 28, 2011

System `medium`
ARM

Place `publisher-place`
London

Company `publisher`
Canonical Limited

OSCOLA `first` reference
    Ubuntu (ARM, London, Canonical Limited 2011)

American Law `first` reference
    Ubuntu, "Natty Narwal," ARM (Canonical Ltd. Apr. 28, 2011).

Chicago Full Note `first` reference
    Ubuntu, ARM (London: Canonical Limited, 2011).

These cite forms are a starting point that may benefit from feedback.

Conference Papers

Conference Paper
paper-conference

Title   title
Merchants in the Temple? The Implications of the GATS for Canada's Health Care System

Author   author
| Epps | Tracey |

Date   issued   *Unpublished*
Jan 2004   *Paper*

Conference/Issue   event
National Health Law Conference

Place   publisher-place
Toronto

OSCOLA first reference

Tracey Epps, 'Merchants in the Temple? The Implications of the GATS for Canada's Health Care System' (National Health Law Conference, Toronto, January 2004)

American Law first reference

Tracey Epps, Merchants in the Temple? The Implications of the GATS for Canada's Health Care System, presented at National Health Law Conference (Toronto Jan. 2004).

Unpublished conference papers should mention the Place of the conference.

Journal Article
article-journal

Title   title
Privatization and Accountability

Author   author
| Trebilcock | Michael J. |

Author   author
| Iacobucci | Edward M. |

Publication   container-title
Harvard Law Review

Volume   volume   *Proceedings*
116   *Published in a*
                                                  Journal

Pages   page
1422-1454

Date   issued
2003

Series Title collection-title
Symposium: Public Values in an Era of Privatization

OSCOLA first reference

Michael J Trebilcock and Edward M Iacobucci, 'Privatization and Accountability' (2003) 116 Harv L Rev 1422

Note the use of the Journal Article type with Series Title in this case.

Proceedings
Published in a
Separate
Volume

Conference Paper
`paper-conference`

Title `title`
Student Editorial Board Members: In the Zone of Proximal Development of Language Learning

Author `author`
Schwieter | John W.

Date `issued`
2010

Book/Journal `container-title`
2010 EABR & ETLC Conference Proceedings

Place `publisher-place`
Littleton, Colorado

Publisher `publisher`
Clute Institute

Pages `page`
142

URL `URL`
http://www.cluteinstitute.com/proceedings/2010_Dublin_ETLC_Articles/Article%20270.pdf

Accessed `accessed`
2012-02-25

American Law `first` reference

John W. Schwieter, *Student Editorial Board Members: In the Zone of Proximal Development of Language Learning*, 2010 EABR & ETLC CONFERENCE PROCEEDINGS 142 (Littleton, Colorado, Clute Institute 2010).

The conference covered by standalone proceedings is identified in the Book/Journal field.

Dictionary Entries

Printed
Publication

Dictionary Entry
`entry-dictionary`

Title `title`
Positive

Author `author`
Bierce | Ambrose

Dictionary `container-title`
Devil's Dictionary

Place `publisher-place`
New York

Publisher `publisher`
Dover Publications

Date `issued`
1993

Pages `page`
96

OSCOLA `first` reference

Ambrose Bierce, 'Positive', *Devil's Dictionary* (New York, Dover Publications 1993) 96

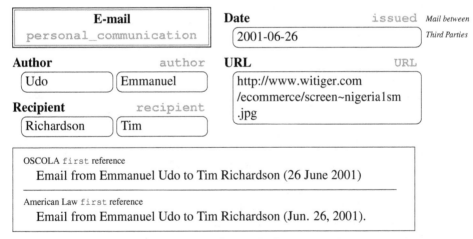

Provide a URL and other available details for online dictionaries.

E-mail

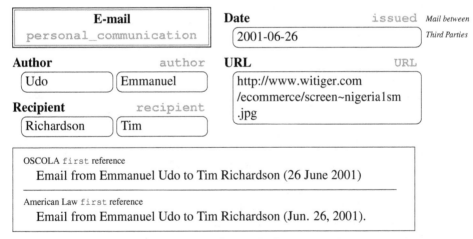

These are a special case of citations to correspondence. Items of type E-mail implicitly send a genre variable to the CSL processor with a value of "email".[91]

---

[91]The same effect can be achieved by using the Letter type and entering "email" in the Type field.

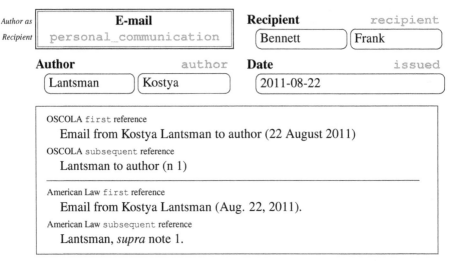

The conversion from a personal name to a placeholder (e.g. "author") or to an empty string is a personalised, style-specific adjustment performed in the Abbreviation Filter (see page 34 above).

Encyclopedia Articles

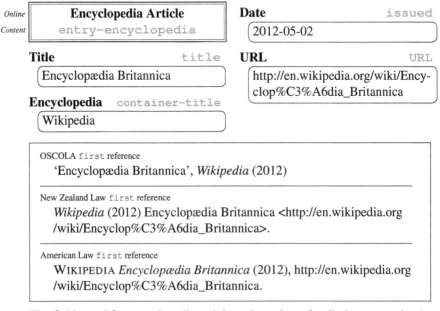

The fields used for encyclopedia articles mirror those for dictionary entries (see pages 62 and 63). In this example, no value is entered for Author or Publisher, but those fields are available on the item.

Films

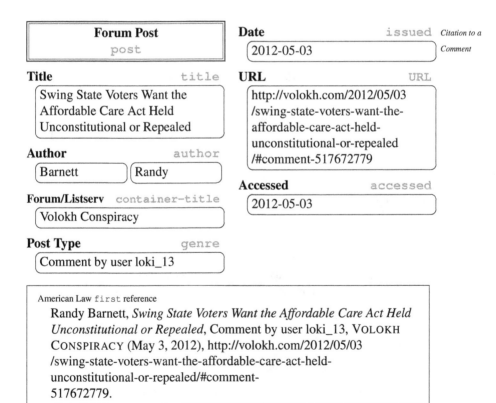

Film	**Distributor**	publisher	*Conventional*
motion_picture	Newmarket		*Release*

Title	title	**Date**	issued
Memento		2000	

OSCOLA first reference
    'Memento' (Newmarket 2000)

The Film type is used only for motion pictures released for distribution to theatres of some description.

Forum Posts

Forum Post	**Date**	issued	*Citation to a*
post	2012-05-03		*Comment*

Title   title

Swing State Voters Want the Affordable Care Act Held Unconstitutional or Repealed

URL   URL

http://volokh.com/2012/05/03/swing-state-voters-want-the-affordable-care-act-held-unconstitutional-or-repealed/#comment-517672779

Author   author

Barnett   Randy

Forum/Listserv   container-title

Volokh Conspiracy

Accessed   accessed

2012-05-03

Post Type   genre

Comment by user loki_13

American Law first reference
    Randy Barnett, *Swing State Voters Want the Affordable Care Act Held Unconstitutional or Repealed*, Comment by user loki_13, VOLOKH CONSPIRACY (May 3, 2012), http://volokh.com/2012/05/03/swing-state-voters-want-the-affordable-care-act-held-unconstitutional-or-repealed/#comment-517672779.

Although a separate type for Forum Post is available in CSL, the CSL-M styles treat it as equivalent to Web Page (page 92 below).

Legislative Bills

Federal Level or Unitary State

Bill
`bill`

Title   `title`
| Research Works Act |

Sponsor   `author`
| Issa | Darrel |

Jurisdiction   `jurisdiction`
| United States |

Legis. Body   `authority`
| U.S. Congress\|House of Representatives |

Assy. No. `collection-number`
| 112 |

Session No.   `chapter-number`
| 1 |

Bill No.   `number`
| 3699 |

Date   `issued`
| Dec. 16, 2011 |

Section   `section`
| sec. 2 |

URL   `URL`
| http://www.gpo.gov/fdsys/pkg /BILLS-112hr3699ih/pdf/BILLS-112hr3699ih.pdf |

OSCOLA `first` reference
> Research Works Act, HR 3699, 112th Cong (1st Sess 2011) s 2

OSCOLA `ibid` reference
> Research Works Act, s 2

OSCOLA `subsequent` reference
> Research Works Act, s 2

American Law `first` reference
> Research Works Act, H.R. 3699, 112th Cong. § 2 (1st Sess. 2011).

American Law `ibid` reference
> *Id.*

American Law `subsequent` reference
> Research Works Act § 2.

Bills are proposals to a legislative body, *prior* to enactment. Note the following with respect to this category of material:

- **Date** is the date of *submission* to the Legislative Body.

- **Assy. No.** is used for the "convened instance" of the body.

- **Session No.** is used for the "session" within an instance.

- **Section** is a statutory locator, as documented above at page 23.

The sample cites above illustrate use of the fields available on this item type in the context of U.S. Congressional sessions.

Bill
bill

Jurisdiction jurisdiction
Pennsylvania, US

Legis. Body authority
Legislature|House of Representatives

Assy. No. collection-number
179

Session Type genre
Special Session

Session No. chapter-number
1

Bill No. number
124

Date issued
1995

Section section
sec. 2

Federal System, Provincial or State Level

Chicago Full Note first reference
H.R. 124, 179th Legislature, 1st Spec. Sess. § 2 (Pa. 1995).

Legislative Hearings

Hearing
hearing

Title title
Copyright Protection for Semiconductor Chips

Jurisdiction jurisdiction
United States

Legis. Body authority
Congress|House Committee on the Judiciary|Subcommittee on Courts, Civil Liberties and the Administration of Justice

Assy. No. collection-number
98

Bill/Doc. No. number
H.R. 1028

Date issued
1983

Title with Bill Number and Committee Name

American Law first reference
Copyright Protection for Semiconductor Chips: Hearing on H.R. 1028 Before the Subcommittee on Courts, Civil Liberties and the Administration of Justice of the H. Comm. on the Judiciary, 98th Cong. 14 (1983).

Note that the title of this hearing is divided into discrete elements of metadata within the Legis. Body field.

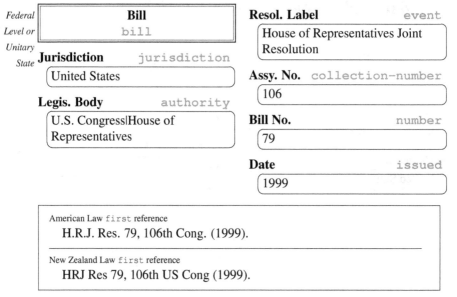

Title and Committee Name

Hearing
hearing

Title title
Transforming the Federal Government to Protect America from Terrorism

Jurisdiction jurisdiction
United States

Legis. Body authority
Congress|House Committee on Homeland Security

Assy. No. collection-number
107

Date issued
2002

American Law first reference
Transforming the Federal Government to Protect America from Terrorism: Hearing Before the House Committee on Homeland Security, 107th Cong. 23–25 (2002).

Legislative Resolutions

Federal Level or Unitary State

Bill
bill

Jurisdiction jurisdiction
United States

Legis. Body authority
U.S. Congress|House of Representatives

Resol. Label event
House of Representatives Joint Resolution

Assy. No. collection-number
106

Bill No. number
79

Date issued
1999

American Law first reference
H.R.J. Res. 79, 106th Cong. (1999).

New Zealand Law first reference
HRJ Res 79, 106th US Cong (1999).

Resolutions are hortatory declarations by a body with rulemaking authority. They use the Bill type with the same field assignments, but are distinguished from proper bills by the presence of a supplementary value in the Resol. Label field.

Bill
bill

Jurisdiction   jurisdiction
Maine, US

Legis. Body   authority
Legislature|House of Representatives

Resol. Label   event
Senate Joint Resolution

Assy. No.   collection-number
118

Session Type   genre
Special Session

Session No.   chapter-number
3

Bill No.   number
836

Date   issued
1999

Federal System, Provincial or State Level

OSCOLA first reference
SJ Res 836, 118th Leg, 3rd Spec Sess (Me 1999)

OSCOLA subsequent reference
SJ Res 836 (Me 1999)

OSCOLA subsequent+ reference
SJ Res 836, 118th Leg, 3rd Spec Sess (Me 1999)

New Zealand Law first reference
SJ Res 836, 118th Leg, 3rd Spec Sess (Me 1999).

New Zealand Law subsequent reference
SJ Res 836 (Me 1999).

New Zealand Law subsequent+ reference
SJ Res 836, 118th Leg, 3rd Spec Sess (Me 1999).

McGill Guide (English) first reference
SJ Res 836, 118th Leg, 3d Spec Sess (Me 1999).

McGill Guide (English) subsequent reference
SJ Res 836 (Me 1999), *supra* note 1.

McGill Guide (English) subsequent+ reference
SJ Res 836 (Me 1999), *supra* note 1.

American Law first reference
S.J. Res. 836, 118th Leg., 3d Spec. Sess. (Me. 1999).

American Law subsequent reference
S.J. Res. 836.

American Law subsequent+ reference
S.J. Res. 836, 118th Leg., 3d Spec. Sess. (Me. 1999).

On the Bill type, a supplementary value in the Session Type field can be used to override the default "Sess." label (or other value, in other jurisdictions) accompanying the Session No. field.

Looseleaf Services

Practitioner
Guide

Book	**Publisher** `publisher`
`book`	Sweet & Maxwell

Title `title`

Cross on Local Government Law

OSCOLA `first` reference
> *Cross on Local Government Law*, para 8-106 (R 30, July 2008)

American Law `first` reference
> CROSS ON LOCAL GOVERNMENT LAW ¶ 8-106 (Sweet & Maxwell, R 30, Jul. 2008).

As publications consisting of a fixed number of volumes that are periodically updated, looseleaf services defy neat categorization. In the CSL-M styles these are handled using the Book item type.

The Date field need not be set in the MLZ item for such services (although it does no harm). Page-specific dates can be provided together with pinpoint details through the word processor plugin. For details, see page 33 above.

Instant Messages

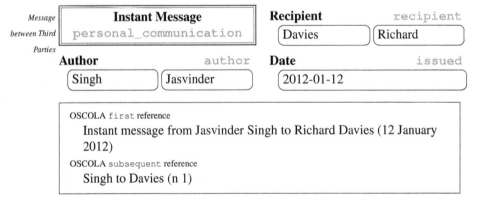

Message
between Third
Parties

Instant Message	**Recipient** `recipient`
`personal_communication`	Davies Richard

Author `author`	**Date** `issued`
Singh Jasvinder	2012-01-12

OSCOLA `first` reference
> Instant message from Jasvinder Singh to Richard Davies (12 January 2012)

OSCOLA `subsequent` reference
> Singh to Davies (n 1)

These are essentially a special case of citations to correspondence. Items of type Instant Message ship an implicit `genre` variable to the CSL processor with a value of "instant message".[92]

---

[92]The same effect can be achieved by using the Letter type and entering "instant message" in the Type field. Also see the Email entry at page 63 above.

Interviews

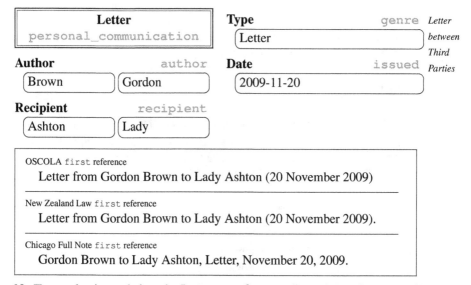

| **Interview** | **Interviewer** | `interviewer` | *Single* |
| `interview` | Coleman | Carol | *Interviewer and Subject* |

| **Interview With** | `author` | **Date** | `issued` |
| Bush | George W. | 2004-06-24 | |

OSCOLA `first` reference
Carol Coleman, Interview with George W Bush (24 June 2004)
OSCOLA `subsequent` reference
Bush interview (n 1)

American Law `first` reference
Interview by Carol Coleman with George W. Bush (Jun. 24, 2004).
American Law `subsequent` reference
Bush, *supra* note 1.

Author initials should always be entered with periods; the processor will strip them if appropriate.

Letters

| **Letter** | **Type** | `genre` | *Letter* |
| `personal_communication` | Letter | | *between Third Parties* |

| **Author** | `author` | **Date** | `issued` |
| Brown | Gordon | 2009-11-20 | |

| **Recipient** | `recipient` |
| Ashton | Lady |

OSCOLA `first` reference
Letter from Gordon Brown to Lady Ashton (20 November 2009)

New Zealand Law `first` reference
Letter from Gordon Brown to Lady Ashton (20 November 2009).

Chicago Full Note `first` reference
Gordon Brown to Lady Ashton, Letter, November 20, 2009.

No Type value is needed on the Letter type for an ordinary letter. See pages 63 and 70 for related examples.

Maps

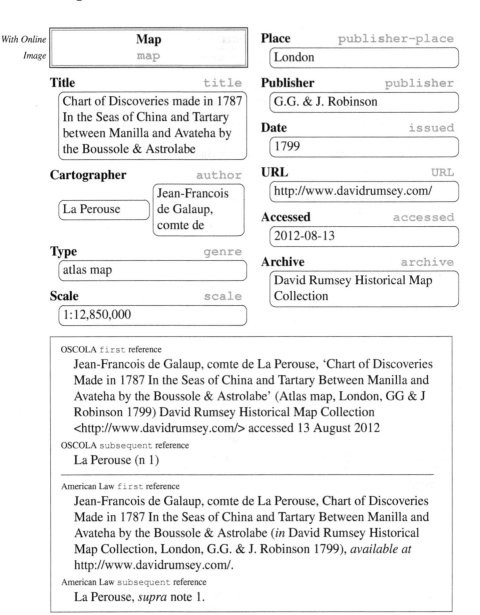

With Online Image

Map

map

Title   `title`

Chart of Discoveries made in 1787 In the Seas of China and Tartary between Manilla and Avateha by the Boussole & Astrolabe

Cartographer   `author`

La Perouse

Jean-Francois de Galaup, comte de

Type   `genre`

atlas map

Scale   `scale`

1:12,850,000

Place   `publisher-place`

London

Publisher   `publisher`

G.G. & J. Robinson

Date   `issued`

1799

URL   `URL`

http://www.davidrumsey.com/

Accessed   `accessed`

2012-08-13

Archive   `archive`

David Rumsey Historical Map Collection

OSCOLA `first` reference

> Jean-Francois de Galaup, comte de La Perouse, 'Chart of Discoveries Made in 1787 In the Seas of China and Tartary Between Manilla and Avateha by the Boussole & Astrolabe' (Atlas map, London, GG & J Robinson 1799) David Rumsey Historical Map Collection <http://www.davidrumsey.com/> accessed 13 August 2012

OSCOLA `subsequent` reference

> La Perouse (n 1)

American Law `first` reference

> Jean-Francois de Galaup, comte de La Perouse, Chart of Discoveries Made in 1787 In the Seas of China and Tartary Between Manilla and Avateha by the Boussole & Astrolabe (*in* David Rumsey Historical Map Collection, London, G.G. & J. Robinson 1799), *available at* http://www.davidrumsey.com/.

American Law `subsequent` reference

> La Perouse, *supra* note 1.

Feedback will lead to further refinements here: the citation forms for Map items are not yet firmly fixed, but this provides a starting point.

Manuscripts

Manuscript
`manuscript`

Date `issued` *Archive*
Document

1937

Author `author`

Johnson | Alvin

Type `genre`

memorandum

Archive `archive`

Horace Kallen Papers, YIVO
Institute for Jewish Research

Archive Loc. `archive_location`

file 36

Place `publisher-place`

New York

American Law `first` reference
> Alvin Johnson, memorandum in Horace Kallen Papers, YIVO
> Institute for Jewish Research, file 36, 1937.

Newspaper Articles

Newspaper Article
`article-newspaper`

Place `publisher-place` *Online*
Edition

London

Title `title`

MPs seek fresh investigation into
News of the World phone hacking

Edition `edition`

Online Edition

Section `section`

Media

Author `author`

Wintour | Patrick

Author `author`

Davies | Nick

URL `URL`

http://www.guardian.co.uk/media
/2010/sep/05/mps-seek-phone-
hacking-investigation

Publication `container-title`

The Guardian

Date `issued`

2010-09-05

Accessed `accessed`

2012-05-05

OSCOLA `first` reference
> Patrick Wintour and Nick Davies, 'MPs Seek Fresh Investigation into
> News of the World Phone Hacking', *The Guardian* (London, 5
> September 2010) <http://www.guardian.co.uk/media/2010/sep/05
> /mps-seek-phone-hacking-investigation> accessed 5 May 2012

Patents

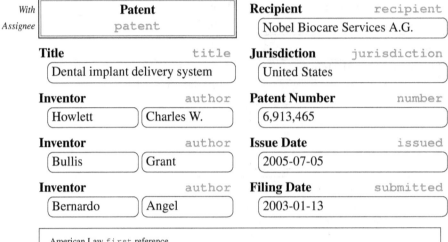

With Assignee

Patent	Recipient recipient
patent	Nobel Biocare Services A.G.

Title   title
Dental implant delivery system

Jurisdiction   jurisdiction
United States

Inventor   author
Howlett   Charles W.

Patent Number   number
6,913,465

Inventor   author
Bullis   Grant

Issue Date   issued
2005-07-05

Inventor   author
Bernardo   Angel

Filing Date   submitted
2003-01-13

American Law first reference
  Charles W. Howlett et al. (inventors); Nobel Biocare Services A.G.
  (assignee), Dental implant delivery system, U.S. Patent No.
  6,913,465, (filed Jan. 13, 2003, issued Jul. 5, 2005).

American Law subsequent reference
  Dental implant delivery system, U.S. Patent No. 6,913,465.

New Zealand Law first reference
  Charles W Howlett, Grant Bullis, Angel Bernardo (inventors); Nobel
  Biocare Services AG (assignee), Dental implant delivery system, US
  Patent No 6,913,465, (filed 13 January 2003, issued 5 July 2005).

New Zealand Law subsequent reference
  Dental implant delivery system, US Patent No 6,913,465, above n 1.

In the Patent type, note the following:

- The Issue Date means what it says; patents not yet issued will have no value here.

- The Recipient of a Patent is the publicly recorded assignee.

- The Jurisdiction field is mandatory. It is used to derive the abbreviation of the issuing state ("U.S." and "US" in the examples), but does not otherwise affect the format of the citation in the CSL-M styles.

As of this writing, the MLZ family of styles implement a single form for Patent items across all styles. Styles may diverge in response to feedback going forward.

Podcasts

Podcast
song

Title	title
PM Lawsuit against former UK Foreign Secretary	

Series Title	collection-title
GlobalNews	

Date	issued
2012-04-19	

Publisher	publisher	*Newscast*
BBC World Service		

URL	URL
http://downloads.bbc.co.uk/podcasts /worldservice/globalnews /globalnews_20120418-1627a.mp3	

Accessed	accessed
2012-05-12	

New Zealand Law first reference

"PM Lawsuit against former UK Foreign Secretary" (Podcast, 19 April 2012) GlobalNews <http://downloads.bbc.co.uk/podcasts /worldservice/globalnews/globalnews_20120418-1627a.mp3>.

New Zealand Law ibid reference

"PM Lawsuit against former UK Foreign Secretary", above n 1.

New Zealand Law subsequent reference

"PM Lawsuit against former UK Foreign Secretary", above n 1.

American Law first reference

PM Lawsuit Against Former UK Foreign Secretary, GLOBALNEWS (podcast, BBC World Service Apr. 19, 2012), http://downloads.bbc .co.uk/podcasts/worldservice/globalnews /globalnews_20120418-1627a.mp3.

American Law ibid reference

Id.

American Law subsequent reference

PM Lawsuit Against Former UK Foreign Secretary, *supra* note 1.

McGill Guide (English) first reference

"PM Lawsuit Against Former UK Foreign Secretary", *GlobalNews* (BBC World Service, 19 April 2012), online <http://downloads.bbc .co.uk/podcasts/worldservice/globalnews /globalnews_20120418-1627a.mp3>.

McGill Guide (English) ibid reference

Ibid.

McGill Guide (English) subsequent reference

"PM Lawsuit Against Former UK Foreign Secretary", *supra* note 1.

When rendering the Podcast type, MLZ sends a genre variable to the processor with a value of "podcast". Also see pages 63 and 70 above.

Presentations

Slide Deck

Presentation
speech

Title `title`
20 Years of Abstract Markup: Any Progress?

Presenter `author`
| Reid | Brian |

Date `issued`
1998-11-19

Place `publisher-place`
Chicago

Meeting Name `event`
Markup Technologies '98

URL `URL`
http://www.reid.org/~brian/markup98.ppt

Accessed `accessed`
2012-05-15

OSCOLA `first` reference

Brian Reid, '20 Years of Abstract Markup: Any Progress?' (Markup Technologies '98, Chicago, 19 November 1998)

Use the Presentation type if the thing cited is the event itself, or content such as a set of PowerPoint slides that do not constitute a finished paper.

Radio Broadcasts

Radio Drama

Radio Broadcast
broadcast

Title `title`
War of the Worlds

Director `author`
| Welles | Orson |

Program Title `container-title`
Mercury Theatre on the Air

Network `publisher`
Columbia Broadcasting System

Date `issued`
1938-10-30

OSCOLA `first` reference

'War of the Worlds' directed by Orson Welles on *Mercury Theatre on the Air* (Radio broadcast, CBS 30 October 1938)

When generating citations from the Radio Broadcast type, MLZ adds a `genre` variable with the value "radio broadcast" to the item. This value may be used in styles to distinguish radio from television broadcasts, which are both assigned the same generic `broadcast` type in CSL. Also see the Television Broadcast example at page 83 below.

Reports

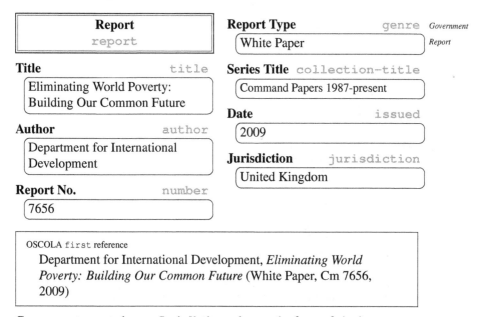

Report
report

Title   title
> Information Management: A Proposal

Author   author
> Berners-Lee | Tim

Institution   publisher
> CERN

Date   issued   *Internal Report*
> 1989-03

URL   URL
> http://www.w3.org/History/1989/proposal.html

Accessed   accessed
> 2012-09-15

> Chicago Full Note first reference
> Tim Berners-Lee, *Information Management: A Proposal* (CERN, March 1989), http://www.w3.org/History/1989/proposal.html (accessed September 15, 2012).

The borderline between Report and Book can be fuzzy, but commissioned studies and internal reports are clear cases.

Report
report

Title   title
> Eliminating World Poverty: Building Our Common Future

Author   author
> Department for International Development

Report No.   number
> 7656

Report Type   genre   *Government Report*
> White Paper

Series Title collection-title
> Command Papers 1987-present

Date   issued
> 2009

Jurisdiction   jurisdiction
> United Kingdom

> OSCOLA first reference
> Department for International Development, *Eliminating World Poverty: Building Our Common Future* (White Paper, Cm 7656, 2009)

Government reports have a Jurisdiction value, as the form of citation may vary by country. In the example, the abbreviation of the value in the Series Title field to "Cm" is done via the Abbreviation Filter (see page 34 above).

Statutes: United States

Enacted Law, Section Pinpoint

Statute
legislation

Name of Act   title
National Environmental Policy
Act of 1969

Jurisdiction   jurisdiction
United States

Date Enacted   issued
1969

Section   section
sec. 102

Date Published publication-date
2006

+

Compiled Code, Section Pinpoint

Statute
legislation

Name of Act   title
National Environmental Policy
Act of 1969

Jurisdiction   jurisdiction
United States

Code   container-title
US Code

Title No.   volume
42

Date Enacted   issued
1969

Section   section
sec. 4332

Date Published publication-date
2006

OSCOLA first reference
> National Environmental Policy Act of 1969, s 102, 42 USC s 4332 (2006)

OSCOLA ibid reference
> National Environmental Policy Act of 1969, s 102, 42 USC s 4332

American Law first reference
> National Environmental Policy Act of 1969, § 102, 42 U.S.C. § 4332 (2006).

American Law ibid reference
> *Id.*, 42 U.S.C. § 4332.

In CSL-M, parallel citations are produced when the item types of two adjacent citations match, the items are of a legal type,[93] and their titles and dates also match.

---

[93] The CSL-M legal item types are: bill, gazette, legal_case, legislation, regulation and treaty.

References to U.S. federal statutes can be given in parallel, with a "logical" or "content neutral" cite based on the structure of the target statute followed by a "publication" cite to a compilation (the U.S. Code) or to the official gazette (Statutes at Large). The two references are stored separately in the MLZ database, and cited (manually) as a pair. It is debatable whether the need to insert the two elements separately constitutes a feature or a bug—the process could be automated somewhat further—but at some cost in flexibility.

Gazette	**Public Law No.** `number` *Enacted*
`gazette`	ch. 395 *Law,*
	Chapter
Name of Act `title`	**Date Enacted** `issued` *Identifier*
White Slave Traffic (Mann) Act	1910
Jurisdiction `jurisdiction`	
United States	

+

Gazette	**Volume** `volume` *Statutes at*
`gazette`	36 *Large, Page*
	Pinpoint
Name of Act `title`	**Pages** `page`
White Slave Traffic (Mann) Act	825
Jurisdiction `jurisdiction`	**Date Enacted** `issued`
United States	1910
Reporter `container-title`	**Section** `section`
Statutes at Large	p. 826

OSCOLA `first` reference
   White Slave Traffic (Mann) Act, ch 395, 36 Stat 825, 826 (1910)
OSCOLA `subsequent` reference
   White Slave Traffic (Mann) Act, 36 Stat 826

American Law `first` reference
   White Slave Traffic (Mann) Act, ch. 395, 36 Stat. 825, 826 (1910).
American Law `subsequent` reference
   White Slave Traffic (Mann) Act, 36 Stat. 826.

In the first cite of the pair above, a proper Public Law No. is not available; the legislative chapter within the session is used instead.

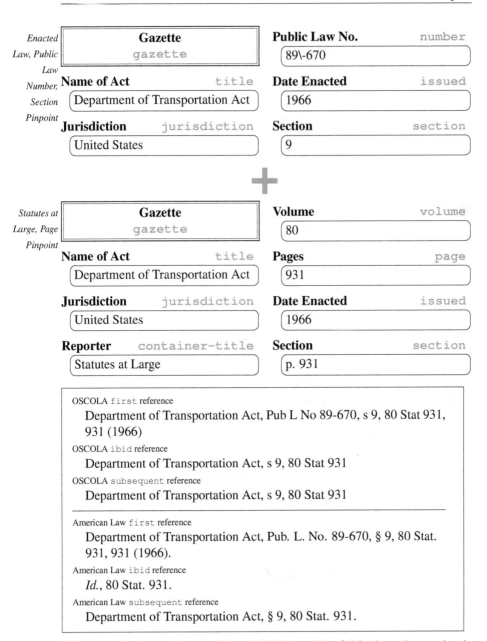

This example shows the use of the Public Law No. field where the number is available.

Gazette		Public Law No.	number	Amending
gazette		ch. 120, sec. 101		Act,

				Chapter

Name of Act   *title*   **Date Enacted**   *issued*   *and Section*

Labor-Management Relations Act   1947   *Identifier,*

         Section

Jurisdiction   *jurisdiction*   **Section**   *section*   *Pinpoint*

United States   sec. 8(a)(3)

➕

Gazette		Volume	volume	Statutes at
gazette		61		Large, Page

         Pinpoint

Name of Act   *title*   **Pages**   *page*

Labor-Management Relations Act   136

Jurisdiction   *jurisdiction*   **Date Enacted**   *issued*

United States   1947

Reporter   *container-title*   **Section**   *section*

Statutes at Large   p. 140-141

New Zealand Law first reference

Labor-Management Relations Act, ch 120, s 101, s 8(a)(3), 61 Stat 136, 140–141 (1947).

New Zealand Law ibid reference

Labor-Management Relations Act, s 8(a)(3), 61 Stat 140–141.

New Zealand Law subsequent reference

Labor-Management Relations Act, s 8(a)(3), 61 Stat 140–141.

Chicago Full Note first reference

Labor-Management Relations Act, ch. 120, sec. 101, § 8(a)(3), 61 Stat. 136, 140–41 (1947).

Chicago Full Note ibid reference

Ibid., 61 Stat. 140–41.

Chicago Full Note subsequent reference

Labor-Management Relations Act, § 8(a)(3), 61 Stat. 140–41.

The first partner above shows the use of the Section field to indicate specific revisions within the amending Act; the second shows use of the same field as a page pinpoint within the law amended.

State Code

| Statute |
| legislation |

Date Enacted   issued

2010

Name of Act   title

Parking Authority Law

Section   section

sec. 342

Jurisdiction   jurisdiction

Pennsylvania, US

Publisher   publisher

West

Code   container-title

Pennsylvania Statutes Annotated

Date Published publication-date

2010

Title No.   volume

53

Public Law No.   number

tit. 53

OSCOLA first reference
> Parking Authority Law, 53 PA STAT ANN tit 53 s 342 (West 2010)

American Law first reference
> Parking Authority Law, 53 PA. STAT. ANN. tit. 53 § 342 (West 2010).

The use of small caps in this CSL-M citation to state-level legislation is triggered by the Jurisdiction field value.

Statutes: Other Jurisdictions

Ordinary Statute

| Statute |
| legislation |

Date Enacted   issued

2008

Name of Act   title

Counter Terrorism Act

Section   section

sec. 1

Jurisdiction   jurisdiction

United Kingdom

OSCOLA first reference
> Counter Terrorism Act 2008, s 1

American Law first reference
> Counter Terrorism Act 2008, § 1.

Most jurisdictions have simpler conventions for citing legislation than the U.S.

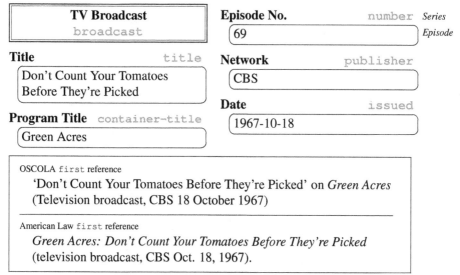

Statute		Section	section	*Regnal Date*
legislation		sec. 1		

Name of Act	title	Public Law No.	number
Crown Debts Act		ch. 90	

Jurisdiction	jurisdiction	Reign	genre
United Kingdom		George III	

Date Enacted	issued	Regnal Year	collection-number
1801		41	

OSCOLA first reference
Crown Debts Act 1801 (41 Geo 3 c 90), s 1

American Law first reference
Crown Debts Act 1801 (41 Geo 3 c. 90), § 1.

For jurisdictions that use regnal dates in statutory citations, the reign is set in the Reign field, and the year of the reign in Regnal Year.

Television Broadcasts

TV Broadcast		Episode No.	number	*Series*
broadcast		69		*Episode*

Title	title	Network	publisher
Don't Count Your Tomatoes Before They're Picked		CBS	

		Date	issued
Program Title	container-title	1967-10-18	
Green Acres			

OSCOLA first reference
'Don't Count Your Tomatoes Before They're Picked' on *Green Acres* (Television broadcast, CBS 18 October 1967)

American Law first reference
Green Acres: Don't Count Your Tomatoes Before They're Picked (television broadcast, CBS Oct. 18, 1967).

When generating citations from the Television Broadcast type, MLZ automatically adds a genre variable with the value "television broadcast" to the item. This value may be used in styles to distinguish radio from television broadcasts, which are both assigned the same generic broadcast type in CSL. Also see the Radio Broadcast example above at page 76.

Theses

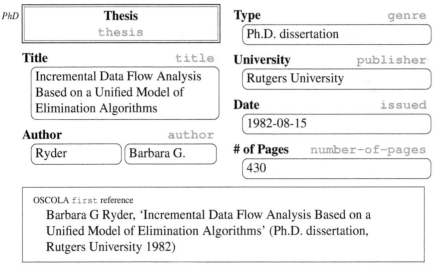

OSCOLA first reference
> Barbara G Ryder, 'Incremental Data Flow Analysis Based on a Unified Model of Elimination Algorithms' (Ph.D. dissertation, Rutgers University 1982)

This type is for unpublished dissertations. Include a note of the degree awarded.

Treaties

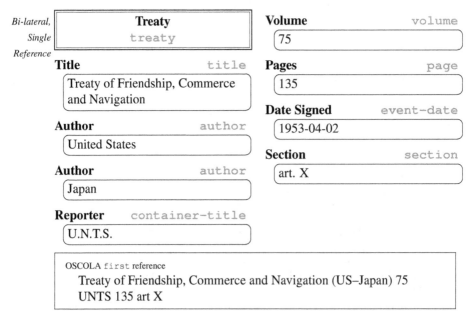

OSCOLA first reference
> Treaty of Friendship, Commerce and Navigation (US–Japan) 75 UNTS 135 art X

Note the use of the Section field in this simple citation to a single reporting service.

Treaty		Volume	volume	*Bi-lateral,*
treaty		4		*with*
				Parallel
Title	title	**Pages**	page	*References*
Treaty of Friendship, Commerce and Navigation		2063		
Author	author	**Date Signed**	event-date	
United States		1953-04-02		
Author	author	**Section**	section	
Japan		art. X		
Reporter	container-title			
U.S.T.				

+

Treaty		Volume	volume
treaty		75	
Title	title	**Pages**	page
Treaty of Friendship, Commerce and Navigation		135	
Author	author	**Date Signed**	event-date
United States		1953-04-02	
Author	author	**Section**	section
Japan		art. X	
Reporter	container-title		
U.N.T.S.			

OSCOLA first reference

Treaty of Friendship, Commerce and Navigation (US–Japan) (2 April 1953) 4 UST 2063, 75 UNTS 135 art X

New Zealand Law first reference

Treaty of Friendship, Commerce and Navigation, US–Japan 4 UST 2063, 75 UNTS 135 (signed 2 April 1953), art X.

American Law first reference

Treaty of Friendship, Commerce and Navigation, U.S.-Japan, art. X, 4 U.S.T. 2063, 75 U.N.T.S. 135.

Note the significant differences in formatting among the styles applied in the examples above.

Tribunals: European Court of Human Rights

Official Report, pre-1996

Case
`legal_case`

Case Name   `title`
Johnston v. Ireland

Jurisdiction   `jurisdiction`
Commission on Human Rights, COE

Court   `authority`
European Court of Human Rights

Docket No.   `number`
9697/82

Reporter   `container-title`
Reports of Judgments and Decisions (Series A)

Year As Vol.   `collection-number`
1986

Date Decided   `issued`
1986-12-18

Date Published `publication-date`
1986

Issue   `issue`
112

> OSCOLA `first` reference
> *Johnston v Ireland* (1986) Series A no 112, 25

Field assignments in Council of Europe items must be followed closely.

Official Report, 1996 and after

Case
`legal_case`

Case Name   `title`
Osman v. U.K.

Jurisdiction   `jurisdiction`
Commission on Human Rights, COE

Court   `authority`
European Court of Human Rights|Section I

Docket No.   `number`
23452/94

Reporter   `container-title`
Reports of Judgments and Decisions

Year As Vol.   `collection-number`
1998

Reporter Volume   `volume`
VIII

First Page   `page`
3124

Date Decided   `issued`
1998-10-28

Date Published `publication-date`
1998

Issue   `issue`
95

> OSCOLA `first` reference
> *Osman v UK* ECHR 1998–VIII 3124 [25]

Note the use of roman numerals for the Reporter Volume.

Case
legal_case

Case Name   title

| Omojudi v. U.K. |

Jurisdiction   jurisdiction

| Commission on Human Rights, COE |

Court   authority

| European Court of Human Rights |

Docket No.   number

| 1820/08 |

Reporter   container-title   *Nominate*

| European Human Rights Reports | *Report*

Reporter Volume   volume

| 51 |

First Page   page

| 10 |

Date Decided   issued

| 2009-11-24 |

Date Published   publication-date

| 2010 |

OSCOLA first reference
> *Omojudi v UK* (2009) 51 EHRR 10 [25]

New Zealand Law first reference
> *Omojudi v UK* (2009) 51 EHRR 10 (ECHR) at [25].

American Law first reference
> Omojudi v. U.K., App. No. 1820/08, 51 Eur. H.R. Rep. 10 at [25] (2010).

Cites to international tribunals vary more greatly between styles than cites to national courts. Such variation makes it particularly important to adhere to a common pattern of data entry for a body like the Council of Europe tribunals, given the sometimes arcane wrinkles in this family of citation forms.

Case
legal_case

Case Name   title

| Balogh v. Hungary |

Jurisdiction   jurisdiction

| Commission on Human Rights, COE |

Court   authority   *Unreported*

| European Court of Human Rights|Second Section | *Case*

Docket No.   number

| 47940/99 |

Date Decided   issued

| 2004-07-20 |

OSCOLA first reference
> *Balogh v Hungary* App no 47940/99 (ECtHR, 20 July 2004) [25]

Similar to cases arising from national courts, unreported cases in the European Court of Human Rights are identified by the application number in the Docket No. field.

Tribunals: European Commission of Human Rights

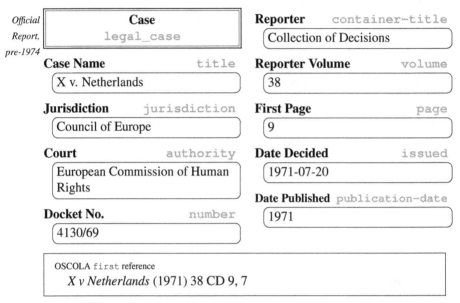

Official Report, pre-1974

Case	
legal_case	

Case Name *title*
X v. Netherlands

Jurisdiction *jurisdiction*
Council of Europe

Court *authority*
European Commission of Human Rights

Docket No. *number*
4130/69

Reporter *container-title*
Collection of Decisions

Reporter Volume *volume*
38

First Page *page*
9

Date Decided *issued*
1971-07-20

Date Published *publication-date*
1971

OSCOLA *first* reference
X v Netherlands (1971) 38 CD 9, 7

European Commission and European Court items are laid out similarly.

Official Report, 1974 and after

Case	
legal_case	

Case Name *title*
Simpson v. U.K.

Jurisdiction *jurisdiction*
Council of Europe

Court *authority*
European Commission of Human Rights

Docket No. *number*
14688/89

Reporter *container-title*
Decisions and Reports

Reporter Volume *volume*
64

First Page *page*
188

Date Decided *issued*
1989

Date Published *publication-date*
1989

OSCOLA *first* reference
Simpson v UK (1989) 64 DR 188 [7]

The official European Commission reporting system has old and new reporters, with the new reporter starting from 1974. In contrast to the neutral forms adopted by many national courts (see pages 53 and 56 above), Council of Europe items always include a value in the Reporter field.

Case
legal_case

Reporter container-title *Nominate*

| European Human Rights Reports | *Report* |

Case Name title

| Council of Civil Service Unions v. U.K. |

Reporter Volume volume

| 10 |

Jurisdiction jurisdiction

| Council of Europe |

First Page page

| 269 |

Court authority

| European Commission of Human Rights |

Date Decided issued

| 1987 |

Date Published publication-date

| 1987 |

Docket No. number

| 11603/85 |

New Zealand Law first reference

Council of Civil Service Unions v UK (1987) 10 EHRR 269 (Commission Decision) at [7].

New Zealand Law ibid-with-locator reference

At [7].

Case
legal_case

Court authority *Unreported*

| European Commission of Human Rights | *Case* |

Case Name title

| P v. U.K. |

Docket No. number

| 13473/87 |

Jurisdiction jurisdiction

| Council of Europe |

Date Decided issued

| 1988-07-11 |

OSCOLA first reference

P v UK App no 13473/87 (Commission Decision, 11 July 1988)

OSCOLA ibid reference

ibid

New Zealand Law first reference

P v UK (13473/87) Commission Decision 11 July 1988.

New Zealand Law ibid reference

P v UK, above n 1.

Both third-party reports and unreported cases of the European Commission work in the same way as those of the European Court.

United Nations: Resolutions

Resolution

Bill
bill

Title   title

Declaration on the Rights of Persons Belonging to National or Ethnic, Religious and Linguistic Minorities

Jurisdiction   jurisdiction

United Nations

Legis. Body   authority

General Assembly

Resol. Label   event

Resolution

Assy. No. collection-number

47

Session No.   chapter-number

49 (Vol. I)

Bill No.   number

47/135, Annex

Date   issued

1992-12-18

Section   section

p. 210

Archive Loc. archive_location

A/47/49 (Vol. 1)

Reporter   container-title

United Nations General Assembly Official Record

OSCOLA first reference

> Declaration on the Rights of Persons Belonging to National or Ethnic, Religious and Linguistic Minorities, UNGA Res 47/135, Annex (18 December 1992) GAOR 47th Session Supp 49 (Vol I) UN Doc A/47/49 (Vol 1), 210

OSCOLA subsequent reference

> Declaration on the Rights of Persons Belonging to National or Ethnic, Religious and Linguistic Minorities, p 210

American Law first reference

> Declaration on the Rights of Persons Belonging to National or Ethnic, Religious and Linguistic Minorities, G.A. Res. 47/135, Annex, U.N. GAOR, 47th, Sess., Supp. No. 49 (Vol. I), U.N. Doc. A/47/49 (Vol. 1), at 210 (Dec. 18, 1992).

American Law subsequent reference

> G.A. Resolution 47/135, Annex, *supra* note 1, at 210.

Support for UN documents is at an early stage in the CSL-M styles, but resolutions are covered, and the cite form illustrated above has a certain degree of flexibility. The example illustrates the field assignments on which further development will depend.

Video Recordings

Video Recording		Studio	publisher	*Indie*
video		Federal Judicial Center		*Videotape*

Title	title
Orientation Seminar for Federal Judicial Law Clerks	

Studio *publisher*

Federal Judicial Center

Date *issued*

1998

URL *URL*

http://www.youtube.com/watch?v=LI3Id1FMaqs

Format *medium*

Videotape

Accessed *accessed*

2012-05-02

Volume *volume*

Part 1

OSCOLA first reference

'Orientation Seminar for Federal Judicial Law Clerks', Part 1 (Videotape, Federal Judicial Center 1998) <http://www.youtube.com/watch?v=LI3Id1FMaqs> accessed 2 May 2012

Video Recording is used for videos produced by an organisation (the Studio), but not published through the theatre distribution chain. Films released to theatres should be set to the Film type (see page 65 above).

Video Recording		Date	issued	*Direct-to-*
video		2012-04-28		*Web*

Title *title*

Multilingual Zotero variant (MLZ) with OpenCongress.org

Website Title *container-title*

YouTube

Director *author*

Bennett | Frank

URL *URL*

http://www.youtube.com/watch?v=NK0hNDhqbSM

OSCOLA first reference

Frank Bennett, 'Multilingual Zotero Variant (MLZ) with OpenCongress.org', *YouTube* (28 April 2012) <http://www.youtube.com/watch?v=NK0hNDhqbSM>

American Law first reference

Frank Bennett, *Multilingual Zotero variant (MLZ) with OpenCongress.org*, YOUTUBE (Apr. 28, 2012), http://www.youtube.com/watch?v=NK0hNDhqbSM.

Direct-to-Web content is distinguished by the absence of a Studio.

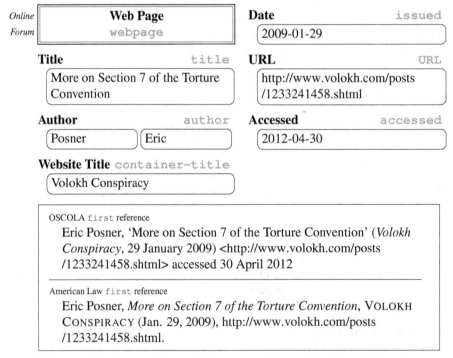

Television
Series
Episode on
DVD

TV Broadcast
broadcast

Format   medium
DVD

Title   title
Tabula Rasa

Network   publisher
NBC

Program Title
container-title
Law & Order

Date   issued
1999-04-20

American Law first reference
Law & Order: Tabula Rasa (DVD, television broadcast, NBC Apr. 20, 1999).

Apart from the "DVD" value in the Format field, the type and fields used for this example are identical to the TV Broadcast example (page 83 above).

Web Pages

Online
Forum

Web Page
webpage

Date   issued
2009-01-29

Title   title
More on Section 7 of the Torture Convention

URL   URL
http://www.volokh.com/posts/1233241458.shtml

Author   author
Posner   Eric

Accessed   accessed
2012-04-30

Website Title container-title
Volokh Conspiracy

OSCOLA first reference
Eric Posner, 'More on Section 7 of the Torture Convention' (*Volokh Conspiracy*, 29 January 2009) <http://www.volokh.com/posts/1233241458.shtml> accessed 30 April 2012

American Law first reference
Eric Posner, *More on Section 7 of the Torture Convention*, VOLOKH CONSPIRACY (Jan. 29, 2009), http://www.volokh.com/posts/1233241458.shtml.

The example above could equally be cast as a Forum Post item. For web content generally, the item should contain as much information as possible about the target site and page.

Appendix B

Field Examples

This section provides descriptions of the MLZ item fields, and guidance for manual entry of data or the construction of site translators. Under each field heading, item types on which a field is available are signified by ☞. Where a field is available on the majority of types, those on which it is *not* available are signified by 🖘.

of Pages

☞ *Book, Classic, Manuscript, Thesis*

Use this field for the total page count of the work. This information is used in some citation styles, and may be useful when generating publication lists.

Example

Non-numeric or mixed-text values may be rendered when a style calls for it, and will look odd in the context of a citation.

# of Pages	number-of-pages
Unknown	

Example

This value is ordinarily a single integer.

# of Pages	number-of-pages
127	

of Volumes

☞ *Audio Recording, Book, Book Section, Dictionary Entry, Encyclopedia Article, Hearing, Video Recording*

This field holds the number of volumes in a multi-volume work, or the number of disks or cassettes in a multimedia publication.

Example

As with # of Pages above, when used, this field normally contains a single integer.

# of Volumes	number-of-volumes
7	

Abstract

🖝 *All types*

The Abstract does not ordinarily appear in citations, but may be used to produce annotated bibliographies.

Example

The text should describe the entry in terms suitable for publication. (The text in this example was drawn from `http://en.wikipedia.org/wiki/Worzel_Gummidge`.)

Abstract   abstract

> Worzel Gummidge was a scarecrow that could come to life. He befriended John and Susan, two children who often had to cover up after him.

Accessed

🖝 *All types*

For mutable sources that also have an address in the URL field, the Accessed field should contain the date on which the source was last viewed. The date is not updated automagically; it should be adjusted manually as appropriate. As this applies to mutable sources, a database may contain multiple entries relating to a single address, representing its content at different points in time.

Example

See the Date field examples beginning at page 103 below for guidance on recognised date formats.

Accessed   accessed

> 2011-11-23

Album

🖝 *Audio Recording*

Example

The second album by Frank Zappa and the Mothers of Invention. The title says it all. Step right up.

Album   container-title

> Absolutely Free

Application No.

🖝 *Patent*

Example

One of several numbers associated with a Patent. Data entered in this numeric field is processed in the same way as for Edition (see page 106 below).

Application No.   pending-number

> 123,456,789

Archive

☞ *[Bill], [Blog Post], [E-mail], [Forum Post], [Gazette], [Hearing], [Instant Message], [Patent], [Podcast], [Presentation], [Regulation], [Statute], [Web Page]*

For rare or unique tangible artifacts, this field should contain the name (not the location) of the archive or collection where the original or an instance of the cited object can be found. For electronic content, the field should contain the name of the folder or search library through which a copy can be obtained.

Example: artwork

For artworks, give the name of the permanent collection to which the cited painting, object or installation belongs. In the database, full names are preferable to abbreviations.

Archive   archive

> Victoria and Albert Museum

Example: rare books and manuscripts

For rare books, indicate the collection containing the referenced copy.

Archive   archive

> Bancroft Library

Example: digital artifacts

Provide the most specific name associated that is likely to be useful to a reader seeking the object.

Archive   archive

> Smithsonian Photographic Services

Example: electronic case reports

Provide sufficient details to replicate the search. The field content can be adjusted via the Abbreviation Filter when generating citations (see page 34 above).

Archive   archive

> 1990 U.S. Dist. LEXIS

Artist

☞ *Artwork*

Artist is the creator field associated with an Artwork. See the Author entry below for creator input examples.

Artwork Size

☞ *Artwork*

Example

The value will typically be a measurement in units. The units themselves cannot be manipulated by the citation processor, but the field content as a whole can be adjusted using the Abbreviation Filter (see page 34 above).

Artwork Size   dimensions

> 15.24cm x 22.86cm

Assy. No.

☞ *Bill, Hearing*

Example

The number of a legislative session. Special sessions within a numbered cycle should be labelled using the Session Type field (page 121 below). See pages 66–69 and 90 above for examples of this field in context.

Assy. No.	collection-number
113	

Author

☞ *[Artwork], [Audio Recording], [Bill], [Computer Program], [Film], [Hearing], [Interview], [Map], [Patent], [Podcast], [Presentation], [Radio Broadcast], [TV Broadcast], [Video Recording]*

Creator names may be entered in one-field mode or two-field mode. Names in one-field mode are treated as institutions. Personal names immediately preceding an institution are treated as joint authors with it. Unaffiliated authors should be entered after the last institution name.[94]

The notes below apply equally to all creator fields (Editor, Translator, Contributor, et cetera).

Example: personal name

Ordinary author names should be entered in two-field mode, with the surname in the first field, and the given name in the second. If the author's given name is known, and not customarily written in initialed form, provide the full name. Styles will initialize names as required.

Author	author
Bierce	Ambrose

Example: name with suffix

Append a "Junior" suffix to the given name in abbreviated form, separated by a comma and a space, and ending in a period. The period will be stripped by the style if necessary.

Author	author
Buckley	William F., Jr.

Example: name with roman numeral suffix

Append a numeric suffix to the given name as shown, separating it with a comma and a space. The treatment is identical to "Jr." above, apart from the lack of a period.

Author	author
Hearst	William Randolph, III

Example: name with "non-dropping" particle

"Non-dropping particles" are ordinarily printed immediately before the surname, but may be ignored for sorting purposes. Enter the particle in the first field as shown.

Author	author
de Gaulle	Charles

---

[94] Such trailing names will be printed *first* when citations are rendered.

Example: name with "dropping" particle

A "dropping particle" is not a fixed part of the author's surname; it is never printed before the surname

Author   author

| Beauvoir | Simone de |

when written in sort order (as in "Beauvoir, Simone de"). Such particles should be entered in the given name field, separated only by a space with no comma.

Example: Asian name

Asian names should be entered in the normal way, with the family name in the first field and the given

Author   author

| 栄 | 我妻 |

name in the second. The name will be correctly formatted in citations.

Example: institution name

Enter institutional names in single-field mode as shown, with all elements of the administrative hierarchy from largest to smallest, separated by "|" (vertical bar) characters.

Author   author

| Ministry of Fear|Awe Division|Shock Department |

Styles will automatically select the elements required for citation purposes.

Authority

☞ *Regulation*

This field is for the Authority issuing a regulation. This is treated as an institutional name (see the institution name example of the previous page for an input example).

Bill No.

☞ *Bill*

The Bill item type is used for a *proposed* rule or piece of legislation, or for a legislative resolution.

Example: simple bill number

Depending on the practice of the legislative body, the number may be a unique ID or (more often) a

Bill No.   number

| 166 |

sequence or other number specific to a particular session or year. Do not include the name or abbreviation of the body itself.

Example: bill number with extra details

In rare cases, the field value may contain non-numeric details. This example is from the U.N. resolution illustrated at page 90 above.

Bill No.   number

| 47/135, Annex |

Bill/Doc. No.

☞ *Hearing*

A **Hearing** transcript may be assigned a number by the issuing body for document tracking purposes, or it may be associated with a particular bill.

Example: bill number

In the case of legislative hearings, the field should contain the bill number as written in the transcript. See page 67 above for an example of this field in context.

Bill/Doc. No.   `number`

> H.R. 1028

Blog Title

☞ *Blog Post*

Example

Include both the title and the subtitle. Styles can acquire the main title through the CSL-M variable `title-main`, if it is correctly set in the **Short Title** field (see page 49 above and page 121 below).

Blog Title   `container-title`

> Informed Comment: Thoughts on the Middle East, History and Religion

Book Author

☞ *Book Section*

Use the **Book Author** field for a book consisting of a collection of essays by the same author. See the **Author** entry at page 96 above for input examples.

Book Title

☞ *Book Section*

The title of a volume containing a cited story, essay, chapter or conference paper. This field is *not* associated with the `title-main` and `title-sub` variables described below at page 121.

Example

Sentence case is preferred in titles; capitalize proper nouns only.

Book Title   `container-title`

> Haircut and other stories

Book/Journal

☞ *Conference Paper*

Conference papers come in three flavours:

1. Those published in a standalone volume with its own title; and

2. Those published as a special issue of a journal.

3. Those presented to a conference without publication;

Use this field for the name of the volume in the first case, and for the name of the journal in the second case. The field is blank in the third case.

Example: proceedings volume

The proceedings of the conference in this example have an ISSN number (1539-8757), but the series has no overall title, so the title of the individual proceedings volume would go in this field.

Book/Journal   container-title

> The 2011 Barcelona European Academic Conference Proceedings

Example: proceedings as a journal special issue

For papers in the volume "Symposium: Public Values in an Era of Privatization", the name of the journal of which the proceedings form a part would be recorded in this field. Alternatively, use the Journal Article type (see page 61 above).

Book/Journal   container-title

> Harvard Law Review

Call No.

☞ *[Bill], [Blog Post], [E-mail], [Forum Post], [Gazette], [Hearing], [Instant Message], [Patent], [Podcast], [Presentation], [Regulation], [Statute], [Web Page]*

A Call Number is specific to a particular library or archive. Accordingly, this value is not normally used in citations, but may find service in styles tailored to generating publication lists or bibliographies for local use. To avoid confusion, the field should not be used for an ISBN or other truly unique identifier.

Example

The field may contain mixed content, so just enter whatever the relevant library lists for the item.

Call No.   call-number

> PS1535 .P5 1973

Cartographer

☞ *Map*

Cartographer is an ordinary creator field. See the Author entry at page 96 above for input examples.

Case Date

☞ *Newspaper Article*

Example

Cases are reported through a newspaper in some jurisdictions. Use this field for the date of the decision, which typically differs from the newspaper publication date.

Case Date   original-date

> 2007-03-09

Case Name

☞ *Case*

This is an optional field in MLZ, as cases in most civil jurisdictions are cited without party names. The field maps to the CSL-M title variable when sent to the citation processor.

Example

Separate party names with "v.": if the style does not require the period, it will be stripped when citations are generated.

Case Name   title

> Smith v. Jones

Code

☞ *Statute*

"Code" may refer to a unit of legislation such as a Civil Code; or it may refer to an official compilation of laws such as the U.S. Code (or the Code of Federal Regulations). Use this field for both cases. The Jurisdiction field will control the format when generating citations (see page 111 below).

Example

The full name makes the entry more accessible to researchers from other fields, in the event of collaboration.

Code   container-title

> Code of Civil Procedure

Code No.

☞ *Statute*

Example

This field is used when citing a compilation, such as the U.S. Code, which is divided into numbered titles.

Code No.   volume

> 50

Committee

☞ *Hearing*

Example

When used, this field should contain the name of the committee conducting the hearing referenced. Append

Committee	committee
Committee on Homeland Security	

a subcommittee, if any, with a "|" (vertical bar) character. The content of this field is appended to Legis. Body, and the combined string is sent to the citation processor as the CSL-M authority variable.

Company

☞ *Computer Program*

Computer programs are often associated with the organization or commercial firm that distributes or markets them.

Example

For widely recognised names (Electronic Arts, Microsoft, GNU), the trademark name is sufficient.

Company	publisher
Nintendo	

Composer

☞ *Audio Recording*

Example

Record the actual composer here (the natural person who wrote the score).

Composer	composer
Zappa	Frank

Conference/Issue

☞ *Conference Paper*

This field should contain the name of the conference (not of the sponsoring institution).

Example: unpublished conference papers

Provide the official conference title; supplementary information is not required for citation purposes, and should not be included. Combined

Conference/Issue	event
The 2012 European International Academic Conferences	

with information on the place and sponsoring institution, this will provide sufficient information to identify the source and its context.

Example special journal issue

In this example, the conference papers form the bulk of a single special issue of a law journal. Although the issue may have other content (e.g. comments or notes, reports on

Conference/Issue   event

> Symposium: Public Values in an Era
> of Privatization

recent legal developments), it is primarily a proceedings volume, and the conference papers it contains can be cited using this type. See the Book/Journal entry at page 99 above for general guidance on the use of this field and the Book/Journal field in the Conference Paper type.

Contributor

☞ *All types*

The Contributor field is available on all item types, but it is not ordinarily used in citations. See the Author entry at page 96 above for input examples.

Court

☞ *Case, Newspaper Article*

Example

In legal case items, name the deciding court in the Court field. As for other institutional authors, list the

Court   authority

> High Court|Chancery

elements of the hierarchy from the largest to the smallest, separated by the "|" (vertical bar) character.

For neutral case citations, leave the Reporter field blank, and give the name of the court in full in this field. The court identifier used in the citation should be generated from the court name via the Abbreviation Filter (see page 34 above).

DOI

☞ *Conference Paper, Journal Article*

 DOI stands for "Digital Object Identifier", a standard code assigned to a work, which can be used to locate copies of it via library resolver services and the like. For more information, see www.doi.org .

Example

This sample DOI will connect to an article about Jonathan Swift. DOI is not just a tech-field thing, although

DOI   DOI

> 10.1111/j.1741-4113.2011.00828.x

scientific styles are more likely to include this identifier in citations.

Date

☞ *[Case], [Gazette], [Patent], [Regulation], [Statute], [Treaty]*

Dates may be entered free-form, but must be standard enough for MLZ to parse out their elements when generating citations or sorting entries. The notes below illustrate recognised formats.

Example: numeric yyyy-mm-dd format

For clarity, simplicity, and portabil-ity, it is hard to beat the form shown in the example. Do *not* use dd-mm-yyyy or mm-dd-yyyy in date fields, since these formats are ambiguous.

Date	issued
2011-12-01	

Example: full month name in first position

A date in the format shown is valid and will be formatted correctly in citations. Month names in other languages may not be recognised (which is an argument for using numeric dates).

Date	issued
April 1, 2012	

Example: full month name in second position

When month names are used, the elements can be in the order shown in the example.

Date	issued
1 April 2012	

Example: abbreviated month

Month names may be abbreviated to as few as three characters as shown. Commas are ignored.

Date	issued
Apr. 1 2012	

Example: dates BC or BCE

Dates before the reference date of the Gregorian calendar should be indicated by appending "BC" or "BCE" separated by a space.

Date	issued
100 BC	

Example: Japanese era dates

MLZ has limited support for Japanese era dates entered in the form shown. Their use is not recommended, and support may be withdrawn in future. Only the most recent four eras are supported (明治, 大正, 昭和, 平成); earlier era dates follow a lunar calendar, and will be passed through literally (see below).

Date	issued
平成2年4月1日	

Example: non-Gregorian dates

Dates without a four-digit year will be passed through literally when generating citations. Such dates will not sort in date order in MLZ item listings or bibliographies. For regnal dates in statutory materials, use the dedicated Reign and Regnal Year fields instead (see page 117 below).

Date	issued
Elizabeth 2	

Date Adopted

☞ *Treaty*

This date field specific to the Treaty item type maps to the CSL-M `original-date` variable, and carries the date, if any, on which the treaty was adopted.

Date Decided

☞ *Case*

This date field specific to the Case item type maps to the CSL-M `issued` variable, and is used for the date of the referenced judgment.

Date Enacted

☞ *Gazette, Regulation, Statute*

This date field specific to the statutory item types maps to the CSL-M `issued` variable, and is used for the date of enactment (not the date of promulgation).

Date In Force

☞ *Treaty*

This date field specific to the Treaty item type maps to the CSL-M `issued` variable, and is used for the date, if any, on which the cited treaty becomes effective.

Date Opened

☞ *Treaty*

This date field specific to the Treaty type carries the CSL-M `issued` variable, and is used for the date on which the treaty was opened for signing.

Date Published

☞ *Case, Regulation, Statute*

Statutes, regulations and court judgments disseminated through a commercial publisher may have a publication date that differs from the date of official issuance. This field maps to the CSL-M `publication-date` variable. This field is not available on the Gazette type, since the act of publication in the official gazette generally constitutes issuance.

Date Signed

☞ *Treaty*

This date field specific to the Treaty type maps to the CSL-M `event-date` variable, and carries the signing date of the treaty, if applicable.

Dictionary

☞ *Dictionary Entry*

This is a Title field equivalent, with support for `title-main` and `title-sub` via the Short Title field. See pages 121 and 123 below for details.

Director

☞ *Film, Radio Broadcast, TV Broadcast, Video Recording*

Director is an ordinary creator field, used for the director of a film or other dramatic production. See the Author entry at page 96 above for input examples.

Distributor

☞ *Film*

Example

Mass-market films reach the general public through a distribution chain. Use this field for the name of the distributor associated with a particular instance of the work.

Distributor   `publisher`
| Universal Pictures |

Docket No.

☞ *Case*

A Docket Number is assigned to a case by the court for administrative purposes. It is not a unique identifier (the same number might be assigned by another court), and it does not identify a unique judgment within a given court (because there may be multiple rulings in a single case). The value is used in certain citation forms, including cites to unreported cases.

Example

This is from a citation to the Supreme Court of the Philippines case *Fortich v. Corona*, G.R. No. 131457, 24 April 1998, 289 SCRA 624. In a CSL-M style, the label ("G.R. No.") would be provided by the style: labels should normally be omitted from the field content.

Docket No.   `number`
| 131457 |

Edition

☞ *Audio Recording, Book, Book Section, Dictionary Entry, Encyclopedia Article, Map, Newspaper Article*

This field is for Edition numbers. Ordinarily it will contain only a bare arabic numeral, which the citation processor may refashion (as an ordinal number, for example) when generating citations.

Multiple edition numbers

Multiple numbers may be given in this field, in the rare case of a reference to multiple editions.

Edition   edition

> 1-3 & 5

Text content

If text content is entered in the field, it will be passed through verbatim when generating citations.

Edition   edition

> First Edition

Editor

☞ *Book, Book Section, Conference Paper, Dictionary Entry, Document, Encyclopedia Article, Journal Article, Treaty*

Editors

Enter the editor of a volume or set of proceedings papers in the Editor field. Input requirements are the same as for the Author field (see page 96 above).

Editor   editor

> Wigmore | John Henry

Encyclopedia

☞ *Encyclopedia Article*

This is a Title field equivalent, with support for title-main and title-sub via the Short Title field. See pages 121 and 123 below for details.

Episode No.

☞ *Podcast, Radio Broadcast, TV Broadcast*

Example

The episodes of a dramatic series may be more readily identifiable by title, but if the episode number within the season is known, provide it here. The example applies to the sixth episode of "Knowing Me, Knowing You ... with Alan Partridge", released on 21 October 1994.

Episode No.   number

> 6

Extra

☞ *All types*

Example

The Extra field is for informal comment on the item that does not rise to the level of an Abstract.

> Extra   note
>
> Derived from the work of Lawrence Sterne.

File Type

☞ *Podcast*

Example

This field serves the same role as the Format field for the other multimedia content types (see below).

> File Type   medium
>
> WAV

Filing Date

☞ *Case, Patent*

A date field mapping to the CSL-M submitted variable, used for the filing date of a complaint or patent application. See page 103 above for date formats.

First Page

☞ *Case*

Example: page or sequence number

Enter the starting page number or (for "neutral" citations) its sequence number within the year in this field.

> First Page   page
>
> 23

Format

☞ *Audio Recording, Film, Radio Broadcast, TV Broadcast, Video Recording*

An Audio Recording could be MP3 or Ogg; a Video Recording might be VHS or Betamax; a TV Broadcast might be PAL or NTSC; and so forth.

Example

With the advent of colorization, an entry such as that shown to the right might be appropriate for some films.

> Format   medium
>
> Black and White

Forum/Listserv

☞ *Forum Post*

A `listserv` is a mailing list (such as `LAW-LIB`), originating from the early days of the Internet. Forums are, well, forums.

Example

For a Forum/Listserv title, use the title most readily identified with the site or service where the target reference can be found.

Forum/Listserv   container-title

| Little Green Footballs |

Genre

☞ *Film*

Example

A genre, when provided, should be one readily identifiable to those versed in film studies (someone who

Genre   genre

| Film Noir |

fits that description better than I can judge whether this example qualifies ...).

History

☞ *Bill, Case, Gazette, Hearing, Regulation, Statute*

This field is intended for the procedural history of a case. Information entered here is not used in citations.

ISBN

☞ *Audio Recording, Book, Book Section, Computer Program, Conference Paper, Dictionary Entry, Encyclopedia Article, Map, Video Recording*

Ten-digit ISBN

The classic International Standard Book Number is ten characters in length (the final digit is a checksum to protect against errors).

ISBN   ISBN

| 0679442553 |

Thirteen-digit ISBN

The 13-digit ISBN is a more recent innovation. You can use either in this field.

ISBN   ISBN

| 978-0679442554 |

ISSN

☞ *Journal Article, Magazine Article, Newspaper Article*

ISSN number

This field may be used for the International Standard Serial Number that identifies the periodical containing the cited article.

ISSN

| 0022-2038 |

ISSN

Institution

☞ *Report*

The Report type can be used for reports commissioned by NGOs and other organizations, in which the originating institution is indicated separately from the individual author (if any). Use this field for the commissioning institution.

Example

This is an ordinary field: the "|" (vertical bar) character used in institutional name fields will not be recognised here.

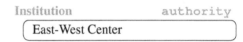

Institution

| East-West Center |

authority

Interview With

☞ *Interview*

Interview With is an ordinary creator field, used for the subject of an interview. See the Author entry at page 96 above for input examples.

Interviewer

☞ *Interview*

Example

When generating citations, the name is normally used as written, as in "George W. Bush. Interview by Carole Coleman, Jun. 24, 2004". See page 96 above for further name input examples.

Interviewer

| Coleman | Carole |

interviewer

Inventor

☞ *Patent*

Use this creator field for the actual inventor, not an assignee. The inventor will ordinarily be an individual. See the Author field at page 96.

Issue

☞ *Case, Journal Article, Magazine Article*

The Issue field is a normal numeric field, and the guidance notes for Volume apply here as well (see page 124 below).

In some styles, the issue number is omitted from journal article cites where pagination is continuous across the volume. This presents a problem, in that whether the issue number should be omitted or included cannot be determined from the item content itself. The recommended solution in official Zotero is to record the issue number in this field, and hand edit the document at the final stage of production to eliminate unwanted issue numbers. In MLZ, items with issue-specific page numbering can be set to the Magazine Article type (see page 44 above). Neither solution is ideal, unfortunately.

Example

A journal issue is ordinarily a simple number, entered as an ordinary arabic numeral.

Issue   issue

    1

Issue Date

☞ *Patent*

This date field maps to the CSL-M `issued` variable, and carries the date on which the patent application was issued. See page 103 above for recognized date input formats.

Issuing Authority

☞ *Patent*

Example

This optional field specific to the Patent type may be used for the specific title of the office issuing a

Issuing Authority   authority

    Patent Office

patent. Do not use it for the *country* issuing the patent; the proper place for that information is the Jurisdiction field.

Journal Abbr

☞ *Journal Article*

The abbreviation of a journal name may be entered in this field. This provides only a single abbreviation for the journal, which may be inconvenient when switching between styles that require different abbreviated forms. The Abbreviation Filter offers greater flexibility, and its use is preferred. When an abbreviation is provided via the plugin, it will override any value in this field. See page 34 above for details.

Jurisdiction

📖 *Bill, Case, Gazette, Hearing, Newspaper Article, Patent, Regulation, Report, Statute*

Example

Several item types used exclusively for primary sources of law require a value in this field.[95] MLZ displays

Jurisdiction	jurisdiction
gb	

the jurisdiction name, but its CSL-M code is used internally. Codes are maintained at the following URL: `https://raw.github.com/fbennett/schema/master/csl-jurisdictions.rnc`.

Label/Publisher

📖 *Audio Recording*

Example

The second album of Frank Zappa's Mothers of Invention was released by the label shown in the example.

Label/Publisher	publisher
Verve	

For precision, include the release number (i.e. V65013) in the Release field.

Language

📖 *All types*

Example: language only

Indicate the language of the source with a valid IETF RFC5646 language code.

Language	language
de	

Example: language and country

This example shows the locale code for German as spoken in Austria.

Language	language
de-AT	

Legis. Body

📖 *Bill, Hearing*

Example

Compose multiple elements of the assembly name, if any, with a "|" (vertical bar) character.

Legis. Body	authority
Congress|House of Representatives	

---

[95] The types are Bill, Case, Gazette, Regulation and Statute.

Library Catalog

☞ *[Bill], [Blog Post], [Case], [E-mail], [Forum Post], [Gazette], [Hearing], [Instant Message], [Patent], [Podcast], [Presentation], [Regulation], [Statute], [Web Page]*

Name of catalog

Use this field to indicate the library to which the Call No. applies (see page 99 above).

Library Catalog   source
Nagoya University

Archive Loc.

☞ *[Blog Post], [E-mail], [Forum Post], [Gazette], [Instant Message], [Patent], [Podcast], [Presentation], [Regulation], [Statute], [Web Page]*

This field partners with Archive, described above at page 95.

Example

The conventions for identifying items within an archive collection are not uniform, but box/file or-

Archive Loc.   archive_location
23/7

ganization is common. The formatting of the data in this field can be adjusted via the Abbreviation Filter when generating citations (see page 34 above).

Medium

☞ *Artwork, Interview*

Example: interview

Interviews may be conducted by email, telephone, video conference, or other methods.

Medium   medium
Telephone

Example: sculpture

Sculptures can be made from various materials.

Medium   medium
Bronze

Meeting Name

☞ *Presentation*

Example

For a Presentation, give the name of the event or meeting here. For an actual Conference Paper use that type instead.

Meeting Name   event
Faculty Development Meeting

Meeting No.

☞ *Hearing*

Example

Use this field for the meeting number of working groups and the like.

Meeting No.   chapter-number

12

Name of Act

☞ *Gazette, Regulation, Statute*

Use this field for the name of an enacted piece of legislation.

Example

Provide the full name of the legislation as applied by the enacting body. If the legislation is more commonly known by its acronym, that can be derived from the full name by the Abbreviation Filter where appropriate. See page 34 above for details.

Name of Act   title

Uniting and Strengthening America by Providing Appropriate Tools Required to Intercept and Obstruct Terrorism Act

Network

☞ *Radio Broadcast, TV Broadcast*

Use this field for the name of the broadcast or cable network from which a program originates. In the case of cable, indicate the content provider: Comcast is not a "network" in this context.

Example

The content provider will be plain from the content of the broadcast.

Network   publisher

CNN

Opus No.

☞ *Audio Recording*

Example

Use this field for the opus number of a musical composition, where applicable.

Opus No.   section

15

Orig. Date

☞ *Audio Recording*

This date field maps to the CSL-M original-date variable, and carries the original date of a musical composition, where it differs from the date of publication. See page 103 above for recognized date input formats.

Pages

☞ *Bill, Book Section, Conference Paper, Dictionary Entry, Encyclopedia Article, Gazette, Hearing, Journal Article, Magazine Article, Newspaper Article, Patent, Regulation, Report, Statute, Treaty*

Example: page range

If the original resource spans multiple pages, best practice is to include the starting and ending pages separated by a hyphen, as shown.

> Pages   page
> 153-172

Example: starting page number

Use a single page number if the original source consists of a single page only, or if the full page range

> Pages   page
> 153

will never be needed in citations ("never" is a very, very long time indeed ...).

Patent No.

☞ *Patent*

Example

Enter a patent number as written by the issuer, complete with delimiters (a comma in this case).

> Patent No.   number
> 1,234,567

Performer

☞ *Audio Recording*

Performer is an ordinary creator field, used for the "author" of musical performances. See the Author entry at page 96 above for input examples.

Place

☞ *Audio Recording, Book, Book Section, Case, Classic, Computer Program, Conference Paper, Dictionary Entry, Encyclopedia Article, Hearing, Manuscript, Map, Newspaper Article, Patent, Presentation, Radio Broadcast, Report, TV Broadcast, Thesis, Video Recording*

Example: single location

The specific location of a city should be indicated only if necessary (when referring to Paris in France, "France" would be omitted).

> Place   publisher-place
> Paris, Maine

Example: places of multiple publishers

Delimit places of multiple publishers with a semicolon, in parallel with the content of the Publisher field (see 117 below).

Place   publisher-place

> Paris; New York

Example: multiple places of a single publisher

When multiple locations apply to a single publisher, do not use a semicolon delimiter.

Place   publisher-place

> Paris and New York

Podcaster

☞ *Podcast*

Podcaster is an ordinary creator field. See the Author entry at page 96 above for input examples.

Post Type

☞ *Forum Post*

Example

In the context of Forum Post, the Post Type field can be used (optionally) to provide a short, one-word description of the type of post cited.

Post Type   genre

> Comment

Presenter

☞ *Presentation*

Presenter is an ordinary creator field, used for the "author" of a presentation. See the Author entry at page 96 above for input examples.

Priority Date

☞ *Patent*

Priority date

This field specific to the Patent type carries the "priority date" of the patent, if applicable.

Priority Date   original-date

> 2001-05-17

Priority Numbers

☞ *Patent*

Example

This field is for a comma-delimited list of standard priority numbers.

Priority Numbers   rank-number

NL19981010536,GB20070006120

Program Title

☞ *Radio Broadcast, TV Broadcast*

Television and radio programs have names. The name of the program (not the episode) should be entered in this field.

Example

A BBC program by the memorable Keith Floyd.

Program Title   container-title

Far Flung Floyd

Programmer

☞ *Computer Program*

The author of a Computer Program is its Programmer. See the Author entry at page 96 above for input examples.

Public Law No.

☞ *Gazette, Regulation, Statute*

Example

A backslash prevents a hyphen from rendering as an en-dash. This field is ordinarily used for a law num-

Public Law No.   number

87\-195

ber, but may be used for other values in special cases. See page 79 above for such an example.

Publication

☞ *Journal Article, Magazine Article, Newspaper Article*

Example

Even in a world of standardised metadata, some journals are more equal than others.

Publication   container-title

Journal of Irreproducible Results

Publisher

☞ *Book, Book Section, Case, Conference Paper, Dictionary Entry, Document, Encyclopedia Article, Hearing, Map, Podcast, Regulation, Statute, Treaty*

Example: single publisher

Give the full name of the publisher if available.

Publisher   publisher

> Cambridge University Press

Example: multiple publishers

For multiple publishers, delimit with a semicolon, in parallel with the Place field (see page 114 above).

Publisher   publisher

> Benn; Barnes and Noble

Recipient

☞ *E-mail, Instant Message, Letter, Patent*

Recipient is an ordinary creator field. See page 96 above for input examples.

Regnal Year

☞ *Statute*

Example

Use this field for the regnal year of the Reign in which the cited Statute was promulgated.

Regnal Year   collection-number

> 10

Reign

☞ *Case, Statute*

Example

Use this field for the name of the monarch or era used to date the cited Case or Statute, where appropriate.

Reign   genre

> Edward III

Release

☞ *Audio Recording*

Example

There may be several releases of an Audio Recording with different liner notes, etc.

Release   edition

> V65013

Report No.

☞ *Report*

Example

The identifier associated with a report might be more than a number.

Report No.   number

SC-CCAMLR-WG-FSA02.51

Report Type

☞ *Report*

Example

This field can be used to provide a short descriptive phrase indicating the type of the report.

Report Type   genre

Annual Report

Reporter

☞ *Bill, Case, Gazette, Hearing, Regulation, Treaty*

Example

Enter the full title of the case reporter. The title can be abbreviated via the Abbreviation Filter (see page 34). For "neutral" citations, this field is left blank.

Reporter   container-title

All England Reports

Reporter Volume

☞ *Case*

The Volume field for case reporters. See page 125 below for the related Year as Vol. field.

Resol. Label

☞ *Bill, Hearing*

Example

See pages 68, 69 and 90 above for examples of this field in context.

Resol. Label   event

Senate Joint Resolution

Reviewed Author

☞ *Document, Journal Article, Magazine Article, Newspaper Article, Treaty*

Example

This field can be used for the author of a work, when citing a review article. Style support for review articles is not yet available, but will come on stream in due course.

Reviewed Author   `reviewed-author`

| Wilde | Oscar |

Running Time

☞ *Audio Recording, Film, Podcast, Radio Broadcast, TV Broadcast, Video Recording*

Example

Use this field to store the duration of the cited work. There is no fixed style of markup in the database field.

Running Time   `dimensions`

| 140 min |

The Abbreviation Filter can be used to normalise entries (see page 34 above).

Scale

☞ *Map*

Example

Use this field for the scale of a map.

Scale   `scale`

| 1:50,000 |

Section

☞ *Bill, Gazette, Newspaper Article, Regulation, Statute, Treaty*

The meaning of the Section field is a bit different for the Newspaper Article type and for the Bill and Statute types.

Example: newspaper section

Newspaper sections are separate inserts or areas of the paper dedicated to a particular topic.

Section   `section`

| Society |

Example: section of a statute

In the Bill, Regulation, Statute and Treaty item types, a reference may include a pinpoint specifier in this field. In the example, `ch.` and `sec.` are embedded pinpoint labels. Embedded labels are parsed out of the string and localised according to the style. See page 33 above for a complete list of recognised labels.

Section   `section`

| ch. 20 sec. 15(1)(A)(ii) |

Series

☞ *Book, Book Section, Conference Paper, Dictionary Entry, Encyclopedia Article, Journal Article*

The Series field is for the name given by a publisher to a series of related books or journals.[96] Also see Series Title below.

Example

The most common use of this field is for a book series, as in the example.

Series	collection-title
Routledge Contemporary Japan Series	

Series Editor

☞ *Book, Book Section, Conference Paper, Dictionary Entry, Encyclopedia Article, Map, Report*

Series Editor is an ordinary creator field. See examples at page 96 above.

Series No.

☞ *Book, Book Section, Dictionary Entry, Encyclopedia Article*

Example: series number

The Series No., if available, may be a simple number (i.e. 23rd in the series, in the example).

Series No.	collection-number
23	

Example: U.N. Sales Number

For the special case of U.N. publications, enter the U.N. Sales Number in this field, and set "United Nations"

Series No.	collection-number
S.07.II.G.6	

(un.org) as the Jurisdiction (see 111 above). Note that the U.N. Sales Number of a publication is distinct from its U.N. Document Number.

Series Title

☞ *Audio Recording, Computer Program, Journal Article, Map, Podcast, Report, Video Recording*

The Series Title field is for a series of similar articles spanning multiple issues of a journal, *or* for a collection within a single issue (see note 96 below).

Example: article series

This is a series of articles in the Proceedings of the National Academy of Sciences (PNAS), written by newly-elected members.

Series Title	collection-title
Inaugural Article	

---

[96]Both MLZ and official Zotero distinguish between Series and Series Title, following the Journal Archiving and Interchange Tag Set Tag Library (ver. 3.0) published by the National Center for Biotechnology Information (NCBI) and the National Library of Medicine (NLM). For details see http://dtd.nlm.nih.gov/archiving/tag-library/n-trr0.html.

Example: journal section

Conference papers published in a single issue. See page 61 above for an example in context.

Series Title   collection-title

> Symposium: Public Values in an Era of Privatization

Session No.

☞ *Bill, Gazette, Hearing, Regulation, Statute*

Example

The number of a session within ab Assy. No. instance of a legislature (see pages 66, 67, 69 and 90 above).

Session No.   chapter-number

> 1

Session Type

☞ *Bill, Hearing*

Example

Use this field for the label of a special legislative session (see pages 67 and 69 above for examples).

Session Type   genre

> Special Session

Short Title

☞ *All types*

This field is associated with three variables in CSL-M:

title-short The Short Title value is always set in this variable.

title-main When Short Title exactly matches the first part of the Title field *leading up to a punctuation mark*, its value is also set in this variable. Otherwise, this variable has the value of Title.

title-sub When the variable above is set to Short Title, this variable is set to the latter portion of the Title field (following the punctuation mark). Otherwise, this variable is empty.

    All of the CSL-M variables above can be transformed using the Abbreviation Filter (see page 34 above).

Example

The main title of the novel by Kurt Vonnegut. Compare with the Title field example on page 123 below.

Short Title   title-short

> Slaughterhouse-Five

Sponsor

☞ *Bill*

The Sponsor of a bill is its author, at least for citation purposes. See the Author entry at page 96 above for input examples.

Studio

☞ *Video Recording*

Use this field for the entity that controls the content of a release, which (properly speaking) may be a production company.

Example

Production company for the original cut of Terry Gilliam's 1985 film *Brazil*.

Studio   publisher

Embassy International Pictures

Subject

☞ *E-mail*

Example

The text should be in the original form (including misplaced capitalisation).

Subject   title

Check Out The Movie Downloads

Supp. Name

☞ *Case*

Example

Use this field to provide the name of a supplement in hard-copy publishing, such as a pocket-part (see page 58 above for an example).

Supp. Name   genre

Transfer Binder

System

☞ *Computer Program*

Example

A computer program may be associated with several "systems"; provide that most relevant to distinguishing and identifying the target resource.

Testimony By

☞ *Hearing*

Example

Use this creator field for the name of the specific individual giving testimony to a committee or panel.

Testimony By   `author`

| Rand | Ayn |

Title

☞ *All types*

The first-listed field in the Info panel of every item, whatever its label, is its title. It may be empty only on Bill, Case, Gazette, Regulation and Statute.

Example

If the title consists of a main title and subtitle, also enter the main-title portion in the Short Title field (see page 121 above).

Title   `title`

Slaughterhouse-Five, or The Children's Crusade: A Duty-Dance With Death

Translator

☞ *Book, Book Section, Classic, Conference Paper, Dictionary Entry, Document, Encyclopedia Article, Interview, Journal Article, Magazine Article, Manuscript, Newspaper Article, Report, Treaty, Web Page*

Translator is an ordinary creator field. See page 96 above for examples.

Example

Enter the name of a translator in the Translator field. Where the translator and editor are the same person,

Translator   `translator`

| Waley | Arthur |

enter the name in both fields; styles will combine the two roles into one as required, in a style-specific form such as "A. Waley (ed. & trans.)".

Type

☞ *Classic, Letter, Manuscript, Map, Presentation, Regulation, Thesis*

Use this field to record distinguishing characteristics of the cited item.

Example

Include the word "thesis" in this field on the Thesis type.

Type   `genre`

Ph.D. thesis

URL

☞ *All types*

Example

When used, this field should contain a valid URL.

URL   URL

> http://pdos.csail.mit.edu/scigen/

University

☞ *Thesis*

Example

Enter the university name alone here, as it should appear in citations.

University   publisher

> Corllins University

Version

☞ *Computer Program*

Example

The version level at which the author parted company with the Windows operating system ...

Version   version

> 3.1

Volume

☞ *Audio Recording, Bill, Book, Book Section, Classic, Conference Paper, Dictionary Entry, Encyclopedia Article, Gazette, Journal Article, Magazine Article, Regulation, Treaty, Video Recording*

Use this field for discretely published subunits of a larger work. That phrasing is awkward, but a "volume number" may mean different things for different media. In an Audio Recording or Video Recording item, it may be a cassette, disk, or archived computer file.

Example

Practice with this field may vary, but unless clarity demands otherwise, try to limit the content to the bare

Volume   volume

> 42

number or key, without a label, and enter the type of medium (disk, LP, floppy disk, etc.) in the Format field.

Website Title

☞ *Artwork, Video Recording, Web Page*

Example

This one can presumably handle our traffic.

Website Title `container-title`

Slashdot

Website Type

☞ *Blog Post, Web Page*

Citing dynamic sources on the Web is a descriptive challenge. This field provides a space for entering a (preferably terse) category description of the site containing the source.

Example

The content of the Website Type field can be transformed for individual citation styles via the Titles list in the Abbreviation Filter. See page 34 for details.

Website Type `genre`

Auction site

Year As Vol.

☞ *Case*

Year as periodical volume

Where a periodical source (such as a case reporter) uses the year of publication as a volume number, the year should be entered as shown in the example. For legal cases, the date of *decision* should also be entered in the Date field.

Year As Vol. `collection-number`

1984

Appendix C

CSL-M Variables by Type

Index

www.ingramcontent.com/pod-product-compliance
Lightning Source LLC
Chambersburg PA
CBHW071208050326
40689CB00011B/2274